POWER, POLES & PLATELAYING

KEEPING THE MANX ELECTRIC RAILWAY ON TRACK

GEORGE HOBBS

Loaghtan Books
Caardee
Dreemskerry Hill
Maughold
Isle of Man
IM7 1BE

Published by Loaghtan Books

First published: April 2019

Typesetting and origination by:
Loaghtan Books

Printed and bound by:
Latimer Trend

Website: www.loaghtanbooks.com

ISBN: 978 1 908060 23 5

For Bill Smith
in memory of Thie ny Claghan

Front cover: Just north of the Ballure level crossing the wire car, number 52, and the cherry picker are attending to the overhead. The MER season finished two days earlier and refurbishment work has started on Ballure viaduct, behind the photographer. The overhead is being removed and will not be replaced until new tracks have been laid across the rejuvenated bridge and the level crossing in late March of the following year *(4 November 2014)*

Rear cover: A contractor's road-railer vehicle is working at Thalloo Mitchell, just north of Dhoon Quarry. Concrete sleepers are being installed on the freshly-placed ballast which will underly the far track. More sleepers are about to be collected from the stockpile by the quarry siding a short distance away. The engineers' surveying equipment assists them in the precise placement of the new track *(11 February 2019)*

Title page: Railway maintenance traditionally relied on manual labour. Judging from the old rails on the left, the southbound line has been relaid near Dumbell's Row in Laxey. Picks and shovels are wielded by the gang as ballast packing takes place. Car 1, with makeshift windscreens, waits on the other track with a wagon load of new sleepers *(Courtesy Travel Lens Photographic, 1970s)*

CONTENTS

INTRODUCTION

The Manx Electric Railway (MER) and the Snaefell Mountain Railway (SMR) are rightly renowned for their historic Victorian and Edwardian fleet of tramcars. Splendid though the rolling stock is, the railways have never been just about the trams themselves. The eighteen miles of the MER connecting Douglas with Ramsey, and the five miles of the SMR between Laxey and the summit, have major elements of infrastructure with associated asset management requirements. These include the trackbed foundations, the permanent way and its supporting structures, the overhead line equipment, the power supply, the station buildings and a host of other items, all of which are essential to enable the historic trams to run at all, let alone provide a safe and efficient public service.

The infrastructure includes a wide range of items ranging from the obvious major assets such as the viaducts at Ballure, Laxey and Groudle Glen, the car sheds at Laxey and Derby Castle, down to the simple shelters provided at some of the minor wayside stops. From an enthusiast's point of view, maintaining the many miles of fencing and hedgerow, controlling the ever encroaching undergrowth, clearing the weeds from the ballast and keeping the drains clear are often taken for granted, but these tasks are fundamental to keeping the lines safe, presentable and passable.

This book examines the history behind the essential infrastructure of the lines and attempts to balance the civil and structural engineering that is no less essential to running this, or indeed any, railway, with the more obvious electrical and mechanical engineering that lies behind the construction and maintenance of the tramcars themselves. Although the trams appear to be frozen in time, many elements of the infrastructure have been renewed to modern standards but do not draw attention to themselves. The trams and the infrastructure are complementary: after all, no infrastructure - no tramway and no service.

Detailed information on the passenger rolling stock is available in many other publications referenced in the bibliography and is not part of the current work.

CHAPTER 1

STRUCTURES

On a random visit to the Manx Electric Railway a visitor is likely to be greeted with the sight of one of the many structures that exist along the route. Especially at the major stations there is a high probability of finding a waiting and welcoming tramcar, but this can never be guaranteed, whereas the immovable infrastructure will always be waiting to serve the intending passenger.

This chapter focuses on the different types of structure that meet the eye. Rather than a geographical journey along the line these are grouped into generic types which will assist in the identification of similarities or differences between the items.

MAJOR STATIONS

The stations on the Manx Electric Railway are very different in character. Generally the facilities are simple except at a few of the more important points along the line. In the country districts the presence of a stop is often only indicated by a flag fixed to an adjacent traction pole. Between Douglas and Laxey simple shelters are usually provided, but the northern section is less well catered for. It might be expected that the facilities at Douglas would be more befitting of the island's capital, but even here a compact wooden ticket office, a shared bus shelter and a few wooden benches suffice.

The major station buildings are located at the junction with the Snaefell Mountain Railway at Laxey, about eight miles north of Douglas, and the northern terminus at Ramsey, a further ten miles along the coast. By passenger usage, if not by buildings, Douglas (Derby Castle) qualifies as a major station.

Derby Castle

The booking office at Derby Castle dates from 1897 and comprises a wooden hut, set on the landward side of the departure road, with ticket windows. The plain wood has been given a 'rustic' appearance by the process of nailing split logs to the planking. The adjacent waiting shelter is of more recent construction and is formed of a large green painted steel and glass 'bus stop' design placed across the end of the tracks. 'Bus stop' is indeed the correct description as it also serves as the waiting area for the bus services on the promenade which pass Derby Castle

The rustic hut which welcomes travellers at Derby Castle: the start of many an enjoyable journey. Since 7 September 2018 it carries a commemorative plaque, unveiled by the Lieutenant Governor, Sir Richard Gozney, marking the MER's 125th anniversary (21 May 2015)

Laxey station with tunnel car 9 with an evening service to Douglas. The station master's office is on the right of the building, with the ticket office next to it. The café and waiting room are to the left. Toilets are at the back of the building (18 July 2014)

on their way between Lower Douglas and Onchan. As Derby Castle is also the northern end of the Douglas Horse Tramway this could be considered a multi-modal transport interchange.

Laxey Station

Laxey is the hub of the electric tramway operations. The Manx Electric Railway reaches this point after eight miles (30 minutes running time) from Douglas and takes another ten miles (45 minutes) for the trams to reach the end of the line at Ramsey. Laxey is the junction with the Snaefell Mountain Railway and the two lines share a spacious station near the centre of the village. The summit of Snaefell is a five mile ride away and can be reached in about 30 minutes from Laxey. The mountain line is laid to a broader gauge (3’-6”, 1067mm) than the MER’s 3’-0” (914mm), precluding through running, and passengers to or from the mountain line must change cars here.

Laxey Station looking towards Douglas. The pre-2014 trackwork and the original rustic sales huts are still in place. (21 May 2009)

The station master at Laxey is in charge of the day-to-day running of both lines and all traffic movements and passenger numbers are reported to him by the tram conductors over the radio. All other things being equal, the Snaefell service is more likely to be subject to variations in demand: on a bright clear day the passenger potential for trips up and down the mountain is far higher and extra cars may be dispatched accordingly. Organized tours may have reserved cars which are interspersed with the scheduled service cars. Unlike some mountain railways there is no restriction as to which service ascending passengers must return on, so occasionally additional empty cars may need to be sent up to clear the mountain at the end of the afternoon. On some days the summit hotel offers evening dining experiences with reserved trams running a late evening service. Diners buy combined travel and catering tickets for these services: the trams remaining at the summit during dinner.

The Laxey station building is a single-storey wooden-framed structure situated on the sea side of the line. It houses the station master’s and ticket offices, together with café and toilet facilities. The roof of the station building carries the name ‘LAXEY’ in large white letters; displays such as this were common on railway stations in the 1920s and 1930s as they provided visual location indicators to early aviators. This practice was hurriedly abandoned in 1939 as it was realised that the principal beneficiary would now be the Luftwaffe and that assisting the enemy with target location was not such a good idea. The post-war reinstatement and maintenance of the roof name adds a period touch to Laxey station’s appearance.

From its construction in the late Victorian era Laxey always hosted a pair of retail huts near the main station building. Of rustic appearance they had shutters which folded down to

During the Rush Hour on the Railways event over the Easter bank holiday weekend in 2018, Ramsey Philatelic Services were selling postal covers from one of the remodelled huts in Laxey Station (29 March 2018)

make shelves on which wares for sale could be displayed. Similar huts can be seen in old photographs of some of the other stations including Ramsey and the now demolished Garwick Glen station. The MER rented the huts to stallholders who provided offerings of such holiday essentials as sweets and cigarettes. The last remaining original huts were at Laxey: these were removed during the major station remodelling over the winter of 2013-4 and dumped a short distance away on railway land on the south side of the Glen Roy viaduct for a time. After more than a hundred years of exposure to the refreshing Manx rain the wood had deteriorated and major repair work was needed before they could be reinstalled after completion of the new surfacing in the station itself. Although the huts contribute to the atmosphere of the station they are now rarely used as sales outlets.

The bar of The Mines in the form of MER car 9. Anyone ringing the bell must buy a round (2 February 2014)

Laxey station also features a selection of rustic wooden benches, manufactured by local craftsmen at the time of the 2013-4 remodelling, in a style matching those seen in old photographs. The benches were funded by Laxey Village Commissioners and a few private individuals and add to the period atmosphere far more than modern mass-produced equivalents would have done. Adjacent to the station is a public house currently named 'The Mines': refurbished around 2016, it was previously 'The Mines Tavern' having once been 'The Station Hotel'. The bar of 'The Mines' is constructed to look like the side of a Manx Electric Railway tram and bears the number '9' on the end. A collection of old photographs of the MER may be seen in the bar area. 'The Mines' was originally the residence of the captain of the nearby Laxey Mine and the area between the tavern and Christ Church was the house's garden. The garden was appropriated by the tramway for the new Laxey station when the line was extended across Glen Roy *en route* for Ramsey. Part of the captain's house was sacrificed to make way for the new tram tracks.

Laxey Goods Shed, currently, with restored Van 16 outside. Despite appearances, the track to the shed is no longer connected to the running line (Sara Goodwins, 23 May 2015)

Just beyond the 'The Mines', at the Ramsey end of the station, is the former Laxey goods shed, a wooden framed structure with corrugated iron cladding. Until the 2013-4 remodelling of the station and its tracks, a pair of sidings led off the southbound line here, one of which ran through the shed while the other lay alongside. Car sets awaiting returning passengers from Snaefell were often parked beside the shed. In the days when goods traffic was carried in wagons, the shed permitted the loading or unloading of items in the dry environment inside. Part of the remodelling works added a new siding between 'The Mines' and the station building: the sidings near the goods shed being disconnected. As it dates from the time of the Ramsey extension, not surprisingly, the goods shed had a number of similarities in style and construction with the former Ramsey car shed. Although the siding outside the shed is disconnected some freight stock may usually be found there as it is a work area for the locally-based preservationists of the Laxey and Lonan Heritage Trust.

Ramsey Station

The current station building at Ramsey is a single-storey brick structure with a covered walkway surrounding it, tucked under the eaves. The interior includes a waiting room with benches, a ticket office, toilets and a staff mess room. The building is a relative newcomer having been constructed in 1964, superseding the previous facilities.

The 1964 building that serves as Ramsey's Station. Parts of the walkway were originally screened by California screen blocks. There are plans to replace the building with a bus-tram interchange facility (21 May 2009)

The extension to Ramsey opened in 1899; the tracks entering the town behind the houses of Waterloo Road, with the terminus near the town centre. The original station building consisted of the wooden hut which had been used at the temporary terminus which opened on the south side of Ballure Viaduct the previous year. The hut was re-located adjacent to what is now the Ramsey Heritage Centre at the northern end of the site. The Palace Concert Hall and Ballroom was located on the site of the current car park and, as ownership passed to the MER's predecessors in 1897, staff facilities were duly provided at the rear of the ballroom. The concert hall became the Manx Picturedrome in 1912 and, after modernization, the Plaza Cinema, as popular entertainment moved to the then new medium. The MER sold the cinema in 1938, which continued in use under new ownership until 1974. After being used as a leisure centre the building was eventually demolished in 1990-1 and the site became the present car park. Prior to the station stop flag's removal, it still bore the name 'Ramsey Plaza', an interesting hangover from a bygone era.

The Plaza Cinema loomed over the station site and restricted the sightlines for the tramway's crossing of Parsonage Road. On the far side of the tracks from the current station building, served by a siding, was the Ramsey goods shed. During December 2016 the goods shed was demolished, the site cleared and most of the siding removed. In common with other buildings constructed at the time of the Ramsey extension, the goods shed was wood framed and clad in corrugated iron with an asbestos roof. Latterly it had served as a youth club, rather unimaginatively called 'The Shed', but had formerly served as a small museum for the MER. Many of the items previously located here are now in the MER museum located at the Derby Castle depot in Douglas (see photographs on page 8).

Over the past few years there have been a number of plans, none of which has yet come to fruition, to replace the Ramsey Station with a combined bus-tram interchange. The existing bus station is a few hundred yards away requiring a short walk for passengers transferring between the tramway and buses serving the north and west of the island. Buses serving Maughold (schooldays only) and the south stop outside the tram station. One proposal included relocating the bus station to the site of the tram station with a decidedly non-heritage steel and glass tram shed combined with waiting, café and retail facilities. The proposal to use much of the site of the Ramsey car shed and the car park located

Left: the contractor's equipment is parked outside the former Ramsey Goods Shed, demolition will start shortly (23 November 2016)

Below: a couple of weeks later the task is nearly complete with only the shed's rear wall standing and debris being loaded for removal (9 December 2016)

on the Plaza site as a bus stabling yard met with resistance from local residents who were less than euphoric about the prospect of having such a facility on their doorsteps. Integrating the transport facilities outside the TT circuit has some logic, but using a high-value town centre site for bus stabling seems questionable in the twenty-first century where such facilities have tended to move to edge-of-town industrial estates. At the time of writing the eventual outcome is undecided.

In the meantime a less than user-friendly temporary tram station has been introduced on the south side of Parsonage Road (see photograph below). Situated a hundred metres away from the Ramsey Station building, with its ticket office and passenger facilities, this new station had no covered waiting area until the start of the 2018 season, when a metal bus stop style shelter was added. The cramped site is not best equipped to handle traffic at busy times, such as during the TT and MGP race periods. Regrettably this development does not serve the travelling public in the way that any heritage railway would wish to do. The station is identified as Ramsey Parsonage Road, to distinguish it from Ramsey Plaza. Hopefully Parsonage Road will soon be superseded.

CAR SHEDS

The shed complex at Derby Castle comprises an interesting mix of buildings which have been developed and adapted throughout the life of the tramway. Built on land reclaimed from the sea inlet of Port y Vada, which was infilled to create the new tramway and coast road, the site included the first power station, and sheds for the initial fleet of motor cars and trailers. The original buildings lay at the lower end of the site and faced out to the sea. Changing requirements meant that these buildings' usage altered and over the years they have housed a variety of facilities. At present, from south to north, the buildings house the MER museum, the paint shop and the maintenance workshops and stores. With the demise of goods traffic on the tramway, the former freight siding was removed and the goods shed is now the museum. The paint shop, which can hold a single tram, is separated from the workshop to provide a clean environment.

In order to maintain the fleet of historic tramcars the railway has little option but to carry out the majority of the maintenance work itself; with few exceptions the original equipment manufacturers are no longer in business and the supply of spare parts is problematic. Although the trams look authentic modern replacement equipment is frequently installed, for example air compressors and receivers are out of sight on the underframes but still provide air pressure for the brakes and whistles.

Above: the car sheds at Derby Castle, showing, from the left; the museum, which is also used for occasional work such as varnishing; the paint shop, and the workshop with the running shed on the right (13 May 2012)

Right: Derby Castle showing the yard hut on the left. In the middle distance are some pallets of recently delivered wheelsets (3 June 2018)

The sheds located at the top of the site consist of a large running shed with eight tracks which provide under-cover storage for most of the service cars and a number of mothballed vehicles. Some of the original tram fleet was lost in the Laxey car shed fire of 1930, but the majority of the fleet is still on the tramway, although by no means all are currently serviceable and some would require major expenditure of time and money to restore to running order. The present building is a steel portal frame structure on concrete foundations and dates from 1996-7. This single structure replaced a three-bay, wood-framed, structure which had been extended over the early years of the tramway's development during 1893-1906 (see page 10). Nearing the end of the twentieth century the woodwork was in poor condition and it was decided to replace the sheds with a more modern building. Concurrently the trackwork of the depot fan was also replaced: unfortunately the track design was such that this required a considerable amount of rework. Internally the building is divided into three bays which are screened from each other above head height. During the building's construction over the winter of 1996-7 the majority of the tram fleet was parked on the line under tarpaulins to protect them from the worst of the weather. The top shed at Derby Castle lies behind a wall which affords some protection from winter storms but, at high tide, the northern end of the Douglas promenades can experience significant breaking waves which subject the Derby Castle site to corrosive sea spray. Close examination of the steel cladding reveals significant corrosion which may need attention in the not too distant future.

Right: the original wooden running sheds and trackwork, shortly before their demolition, which took place the following winter. Note that the trailer next to post van 4 is wrapped in plastic; the author has no idea why! (Sara Goodwins 10 May 1996)

Below: a similar view showing the replacement steel-framed running shed and the new trackwork installed in the late 1990s (13 May 2012)

Laxey shed

The Laxey car shed is unusual in that it has had three incarnations. When the tramway was extended from Groudle to Laxey in 1894 all cars were stabled at Derby Castle. The original Laxey terminus was inconvenient, requiring passengers to walk into Laxey Village. When the Snaefell line opened the following year, those wishing to travel on the mountain line, whose terminus was adjacent to the current Snaefell car shed, had even further to walk. Costly engineering works to carry the tramway across Glen Roy had been avoided for the time being.

After four years the Ramsey extension was constructed and the original Laxey terminus was superseded by the current Laxey Station. A new Laxey car shed was erected in 1904, at the same time as the goods shed at the far end of Laxey Station, and was a wood-framed structure, clad in corrugated iron which could accommodate sixteen cars. The new shed was adjacent to the site of the original 1894 terminus, on the inland side of the line. This was referred to as a 'new' shed, but it seems possible that this may have superseded a smaller temporary structure. The extra rolling stock acquired up to 1906 (six motor and ten trailer cars) meant that this amount of additional covered storage would have been needed.

The 1904 car shed served until the night of Saturday 5th April 1930 when a major fire, discovered around 10:40pm and lasting until the next morning, resulted in the total loss of the building with the destruction of four motor cars (numbers 3, 4, 8 and 24), seven trailers (34, 35, 38, 39, 40, 41 and 44), all three tower wagons, a mail van and a large quantity of tools and equipment. Three replacement open trailers (numbered 40, 41 and 44) were supplied by English Electric from Preston, taking the numbers of three of those lost to the flames. These were similar to the original Victorian vehicles and by no means 'modern'. Neither the destroyed motor cars, nor the other four trailers, were replaced as the company's insurance was inadequate.

Left: the maker's nameplate on the end of the second Laxey car shed (9 May 2002)

Below: winter saloon 20 and trailer 40 pass the decidedly rusty-roofed Laxey car shed with a Ramsey-bound service. During this week trams were removed from the shed and taken to Douglas for onward movement by low loader to the former Homefield bus garage. The roof will soon be gone (5 May 2002)

A new Laxey car shed was erected later in 1930, replacing the one destroyed by fire. This was a steel-framed arched-roof structure clad with corrugated iron. It was a standard industrial design supplied by W H Smith and Co (Whitchurch) Ltd, based in Shropshire. (Ironfounders and agricultural and structural engineeers, this company should not be confused with the well-known high street stationers.) The structure contained four tracks and was accessed via a headshunt at the Douglas end of the building. Interestingly, the furthermost track from the running lines was only accessible by running through the shed and reversing back in from the adjacent track. Not surprisingly it tended to house the less active members of the fleet.

Over the years the 1930 shed suffered from considerable corrosion and, in spring 2002, the majority of the contents were removed for storage in the former Isle of Man Road Services Highfield Bus Garage in Salisbury Street, Douglas. (The garage has since been demolished and the site redeveloped.) Cars were towed to Douglas and transferred to a low loader lorry for transport to their temporary resting place. As the roof was considered liable to collapse it was removed, the now roofless 'shed' continuing to harbour a few vehicles dedicated to engineering use.

Six years to the day after the previous photograph, the remains of the roof of the shed now lie in pieces on the floor on the right. Diesel-electric engineer's locomotive number 34 is parked inside, but not protected from the weather (5 May 2008)

Right: the new Laxey shed has been erected and the paintwork is pristine. Meanwhile the permanent way contractors are finalizing the track access to the new facility (21 May 2009)

Below: inside the new Laxey shed car 33 and wire car 52 are ready and waiting should they be needed (24 September 2015)

Finally, the remains of the 1930 shed were removed and another, similar-sized, shed was erected in early 2009. This is also a steel-framed structure with corrugated iron cladding, retaining an arched roof like its immediate predecessor. The shed contains only three tracks, all accessed from the Douglas end headshunt. In place of the fourth track (the one that was reached by passing through the shed and reversing) a concrete hard standing area has been provided. At the time of writing, this area houses a number of unserviceable vehicles stored without trucks.

Depending on the timetable in operation, Laxey Shed may supply cars and, if required, trailers for scheduled services either to or from Douglas or Ramsey. Although this was common practice in 2015-7, following the closure of Ramsey shed, there were no such turns scheduled in 2018. As engineering maintenance is normally carried out at Derby Castle the standard practice is to use Laxey for overnight accommodation. A car which started at Douglas may end its day in the evening at Laxey and return to Derby Castle after a second day's service. In addition, Laxey normally houses the wire car, 52, and an open motor, usually car 33, for use by the overhead line engineers who are based at Laxey. When required, the wire car can be dispatched towards either end of the line in order to attend to overhead problems occurring during normal operations.

Ramsey Shed

The Manx Electric Railway was extended from Laxey in 1898 reaching a point just south of the current Ballure Viaduct, and opened for service on 2 August. The choice facing the tramway was to open that far and capture some of the season's traffic or delay opening until the viaduct was complete and open the line through to Ramsey. As Ballure is only about three-quarters of a mile from Ramsey town centre, and rather less to the Queen's Pier, it was deemed worthwhile to provide temporary facilities within a relatively easy walk of the true traffic objectives.

A temporary tram shed, capable of holding six cars, was constructed on part of the space now occupied by the public gardens on the seaward side of the line. After completion of the Ballure viaduct in 1899 the tramway was duly projected to Ramsey, opening to the public on 24 July. The temporary terminus at Ballure became redundant. There is some argument about whether the tramshed at Ballure was dismantled and moved nearer the end of the line, or whether the building erected at Ramsey was a totally new construction. The date of the opening of the shed near the terminus is obscure, but it is possible that the Ballure shed continued in use for a short while after the Ramsey extension opened. Dumbell's Bank collapsed on 2 February 1900, eventually leading to the financial reconstitution of the tramway as the Manx Electric Railway in 1902. In the harsh financial climate it is possible that economies were made to provide facilities at Ramsey and that the shed from Ballure was relocated.

The careworn Ramsey car shed shortly before its demolition. The overhead wires and bracket arms have been removed from the adjacent track to improve access for the contractor's demolition plant (23 November 2016)

Left: Ramsey car shed undergoing demolition. The contractor's equipment stands over the former inspection pit, showing that about half the shed has now been removed (2 December 2016)

Below: the connexion from the southbound line to the car shed has been replaced with new plain line, with Pandrol clips, so there is no railway access to the former shed site. The contractors are busy clearing the site and all traces will soon be gone (10 December 2016)

The Ramsey shed was a two-road structure located on the south side of Parsonage Road and reached by shunting from Ramsey Plaza station. The timber framework was clad with corrugated iron and asbestos sheets. The shed could accommodate six cars, the same as the Ballure temporary shed. Time had taken its toll on the structure and it was decided that it was unsafe to use beyond the end of the 2014 season. Car 22 was the last service car to be stabled there at the close of the season on the evening of 2 November (see page 14).

In the next few days four items of non-serviceable rolling stock were removed from Ramsey Shed and taken to Laxey. Unusually the transfer was carried out by low loader lorry providing the spectacle of trams travelling along the A2 road rather than along the line (see page 14). The shed then remained unused for a couple of years. Despite the claim that the shed was unsafe, it was host to the engineering diesel-electric, car 34, for a while, following mechanical problems with the locomotive. In December 2016 the car shed was demolished, and the site, including all trackwork, cleared in early 2017.

The loss of the overnight stabling facilities at Ramsey has meant that, since the start of the 2015 season, cars working the first morning service from Ramsey have had to work up to Ramsey rather than backing down from the shed. This has also meant that there are no Ramsey-based platform staff. Depending on which timetable is in operation, the first car from Ramsey will have started from either Douglas or Laxey. Consequently, there is now an earlier morning service on the Laxey to Ramsey section. In the main part of the season the first tram arrives at Ramsey at 09:55 and forms the 10:10 departure for Douglas. When the most basic timetable is in operation, near the ends of the season, the first car from Ramsey to Douglas leaves at the later time of

The last service car to be stabled at Ramsey proceeds to the shed after working the final northbound service at the end of the 2014 season. Inside the shed are long-term stored stock, including ratchet car 14 which returned to service in time for the MER's 125th anniversary in September 2018 (2 November 2014)

11:10, arriving at 12:25 which is less than ideal for either visitors or northern residents. The lack of overnight stabling at Ramsey has also caused an erosion of the late afternoon service as the final northbound car has to return to either Douglas or Laxey for overnight stabling.

ELECTRICAL SUBSTATIONS

The power to the MER's tramway overhead is provided by five substations, which transform and rectify the high voltage AC supply from the grid into low voltage DC for local use via the overhead. The distance between substations is approximately four miles. There is an additional substation dedicated to the SMR.

The substation at Derby Castle is located within the depot complex and does not have a separate structure to house it. Originally the power station here provided low voltage DC current directly to the overhead. The generating plant was superseded by the substation when high voltage AC power was supplied from Laxey power station in 1904 and later from the Manx national grid in the 1930s.

The substation at Groudle housed the last mercury-arc rectifier in use on the tramway. The building, which still stands at the time of writing, is located on private land and closed at the end of the 2017 operating season. The

Below: Ramsey car shed was rapidly cleared of the unserviceable stock following the end of the 2014 season. Ratchet car 14 passes Primrose Lodge, on the main A2 road, carried on a low loader. The tram will be unloaded in Laxey station and shunted to the shed for a further period of storage (Sara Goodwins, 3 November 2014)

Left: the completed Ballameanagh substation showing the new feeder arrangements and the relocated shelter which is now a few yards nearer Baldrine (8 March 2018)

Below: photographed during construction and normally unseen, the back of the new Ballameanagh substation shows good economics as the concrete structure does not feature the decorative stone facing of the frontage (2 July 2017)

stone-built structure is located inland of the line near the site of the old toll house.

The Groudle substation was replaced by the new Ballameanagh installation located between Halfway and Baldrine. This concrete building, situated next to the Ballameanagh stop, is faced with Manx stone to give its frontage a more rustic appearance. The rear of the structure is not visible to passers-by on the main road and lacks the decorative facing of the front. The building adjoins Barroose farm, whereas Ballameanagh lies on the other side of the A2 road, so the installation is sometimes called the Barroose substation.

The Laxey substation lies on the inland side of the line between the Glen Roy viaduct and the Laxey car shed. Power is supplied for both the Manx Electric and the Snaefell Mountain Railways via feeder cables carried on the traction poles across the Glen Roy viaduct. The present building came into use at the start of the 2014 season and is of a similar size to the more recent structure at Ballameanagh. The previous substation, which still stands, is a brick-built structure a few yards nearer the car shed and adjacent to the Rencell Road underbridge. This building housed a mercury-arc rectifier which was decommissioned at the end of the 2013 season. Tours of this building, allowing observation of the rectifier in action, were available to the public as part of the Isle of Man heritage weekends in October 2013, shortly before decommissioning.

At Ballagorry is the sole overbridge on the MER. A substation is built into the bridge abutments on the seaward side of the line. This installation replaced the supply drawn from the previous rotary converters located at the

Above: the substation at Laxey which was superseded at the end of the 2013 operating season. The building remains in use although the electrical supply has moved closer to Laxey station (6 October 2013)

Right: the new Laxey substation is this functional building situated between the car shed and the Glen Roy viaduct. Unlike the similar-sized structure at Ballameanagh the concrete has no stone facing (9 June 2017)

Right: the substation at Ballagorry tucked under the eastern side of the bridge and very inconspicuous (20 May 2010)

Below: the recently refurbished substation at Bellevue is situated above the line on the opposite side of the road crossing from the stop. Note the siren mounted near the top of the end gable. It is part of the island's Civil Defence all-island emergency warning system, and nothing to do with the tramway. Unfortunately (30 April 2017)

former Ballaglass power station about half a mile closer to Ramsey (see pages 32 and 33).

The final substation is located on the Laxey side of the stop at Bellevue, about two miles before the end of the line at Ramsey. It is a brick-built structure with a transformer located outside.

BRIDGES AND VIADUCTS

Groudle

In order to project the tramway beyond Groudle Glen towards Laxey the deep ravine of Groudle Glen had to be bridged. A three-arch masonry viaduct with 20ft (6.1m) spans was constructed to carry both the tramway and the new toll road. From a passenger's point of view the tall trees reaching up from the valley bottom conceal the true depth of the ravine here, but seen from below the scale of the viaduct looming fifty feet or more above can be appreciated to the full. Construction of any of the arches along the line would have been by the traditional method of wooden centring to support the masonry until the mortar had set.

Lhen Coan

About half a mile up the hill from the Groudle viaduct, heading towards Laxey, the road and tramway cross one of the tributaries to the Groudle River, where one of the side valleys of the Glen descends from Eskadale. The bridge is constructed with a high degree of skew. It is a single-arch masonry structure, and the inland parapet is clearly visible from the tramway.

Seen from below, and looking towards the sea, the Groudle viaduct is far more impressive than from track level. The MER overhead is just visible above the parapet (2 April 2017)

Rencell Road

Rencell Road is steep and narrow and is crossed by the MER almost immediately after the Laxey car shed on the way to Laxey Station. Of short span and limited headroom this bridge has been rebuilt in recent years. It now comprises steel I-beams, supported by the original abutments, the load-bearing beams being located directly beneath the tramway rails: this is an elegant solution providing a shallow deck which preserves the road's headroom.

Glen Roy (Laxey)

The extension of the tramway beyond the original Laxey Station near the car shed, towards Ramsey required viaducts across Glen Roy, Minorca Hill and the stream between Laxey and Minorca. The Isle of Man's Tramways & Electric Power Co. Ltd.'s (IoMTEP) engineer for the extension was William Knowles, and the bridge contractor Mark Carine. Not surprisingly the three masonry viaducts dating from this time are clearly the work of the same designer, with ornate castellated parapets featuring on all three which have a strong resemblance to the Groudle viaduct. The first obstacle to be crossed was Glen Roy with the substantial curved masonry viaduct leading to the southern end of Laxey Station.

Left: Rencell Road bridge lies on the station side of Laxey car sheds and has very restricted headroom. This view is looking uphill and, from the courses of stonework it is clearly very steep, about 1 in 8. The minimum headroom is at the upper edge of the bridge, an adjacent street sign quotes 7'-3" (2.21m) as the clearance. The main girders are directly below the rails with smaller beams, some of which are old rails, to support the decking (2 April 2017)

Below: the Glen Roy viaduct seen from the approach road to the Laxey flour mill (2 April 2017)

In crossing Glen Roy, the Laxey viaduct also spans both Church Hill and the access road to the Laxey flour mill (formerly Corlett's mill), which is located a short distance upstream of the viaduct and the parallel road bridge carrying the Laxey New Road over Glen Roy.

The Laxey Viaduct is unusual as it features two very different forms of construction. While the four southern spans are masonry arches, the northernmost span, which crosses the steep Church Hill, required a flat soffit to provide adequate headroom across the full width of the carriageway. A fifth arch would have reduced the clearances, so this span's construction featured a cross-girdered deck. The steel main girders were braced by lateral girders with brick jack arches: a standard form of construction for many rail bridges of this era. Over the years corrosion of the steel girders by water

The Glen Roy viaduct is seen from the south side of the valley. Track relaying works are visible in Laxey Station and a ballast hopper, borrowed from the steam railway, can be seen in the foreground (21 February 2014)

percolation decreased this span's load capacity and remedial works became necessary. Between November 2010 and February 2011 Church Hill was closed to all traffic, the span demolished and a new reinforced concrete deck installed. The bridge parapets were carefully dismantled and reconstructed in an identical form to the originals, so that the rebuilt section has a good visual match with the remainder of the viaduct. The only give away is that the soffit of the span over Church Hill is now a flat expanse of concrete rather than the cross girder and jack arch construction of the original.

The mixture of the two forms of construction provided a challenge to the designers. With a multi-span masonry bridge all the spans act in concert to carry the dead weight of the bridge and its imposed loads. The flat-soffited northernmost span over Church Hill could not be part of this action and the masonry column between the fourth arch and Church Hill is considerably more substantial than the others to provide the necessary strength to the masonry arches. In effect the Church Hill span is a separate structure, although passengers on the tramway will not be conscious of this.

Test House/Minorca Intermediate

On the climb from Laxey to Minorca one of the side streams of the Laxey River is crossed on a masonry arch bridge about a quarter of a mile before Minorca. This is a single span structure between abutments with decorative castellations on the parapets.

Minorca

The viaduct over Minorca Hill, adjacent to the Minorca tram stop, is the third and final masonry viaduct in the Laxey area. Unusually for the MER this is one of the few bridges which crosses a relatively major road, the B1, which connects Minorca Cross Roads to Old Laxey and Laxey Old Hill on the south side of the valley, re-crossing the MER at Preston's Crossing, before rejoining the main A2 road near Fairy Cottage. The structure is once again a single span arch with castellated parapets.

This abutment marks the boundary of the Glen Roy viaduct on the left and the new reinforced concrete span over Church Hill in Laxey. The abutment is far thicker on the non visible face (7 January 2018)

Left: The bridge at Minorca looking towards Laxey. A mechanical digger is on the northbound line as urgent track repair work is underway and the line is closed. A bridge such as this would typically be expected to carry about thirty tons of ballast (6 May 2008)

Below: seen from below, Minorca Bridge is impressive. The route taken by the local electricity supply cables passing underneath with a horizontal arrangement is unusual (26 March 2017)

Ballagorry

This bridge is now the only overbridge on the Manx Electric Railway and was originally built to give a local farmer access to his land. Today it also provides access from the A2 coast road to nearby houses. The original timber bridge, built by Joshua Shaw and dating from 1901, became inadequate to handle modern traffic loads and was replaced by the current concrete structure in about 1950. There are two intermediate piers founded adjacent to the tracks. The seaward side abutment of the bridge includes a substation for the overhead supply.

Ballure

The viaduct at Ballure is the only major structure on the tramway built in steel, and is a departure from the approach used on the viaducts constructed in the previous five years. The valley floor is not flat as the Ballure river flows round a horseshoe bend under the viaduct. For a masonry viaduct three identical spans would have been ideal but locating the piers would have been difficult. The two-span steel structure has a central masonry pier positioned on the solid foundation of the raised part of the valley floor inside the horseshoe. The spans are truss girders with the tracks supported on the top. Extensive use of riveted connexions was made between the built-up longitudinal girder plates and the cross-

The overbridge at Ballagorry looking towards Laxey. The substation is in the left hand abutment (see page 16) almost obscured by foliage (20 May 2010)

The Ballure viaduct seen following its major refurbishment over the winter of 2014-5. Winter saloon 20 and trailer 41 are about to cross Ballure Road on their way to Ramsey. The massive masonry pier and abutment have stood up well to 120 years of service (16 September 2015)

bracing angle sections, typical of many bridges of that era. The girders are 80ft (24.4m) span, 9ft (2.7m) wide and have a separation of 10ft (3m). The bridge was constructed by a non-Manx contractor, Francis Morton and Co, Bridge and Roof Builders of Garston, Lancashire, with the components shipped to the island for erection; the engineer was William Knowles. Francis Morton and Company Ltd was formed in 1853 and based in Naylor Road, Liverpool, moving to Garston (Lancashire) in 1888. Francis Morton also constructed the main girders of the Liverpool Overhead Railway. In June 1898 the company was purchased by a consortium from Manchester and Liverpool, including John Wood, who became the company's new chairman. The contractor and engineer are commemorated on a plaque affixed to the Ramsey end abutment on the land side of the line.

Steel bridges benefit from a higher speed of erection, with a reduced amount of heavy temporary works and lower initial cost. Their main disadvantage is the battle against strength-sapping corrosion. Advances in coating technology mean that paint with a lifetime approaching thirty years is now available: the quip about the task of painting the Forth Bridge being a never-ending labour no longer being true. The task is no longer continuous but still recurrent and this certainly applies to the MER's Ballure viaduct. Once the last tram had passed over at the end of the 2014 season the viaduct was subjected to a considerable programme of work involving replacement of corroded sections with new, now with high strength bolted connexions in place of hot-driven rivets. The old paint was stripped away, and recoating in smart green paint completed the work on the structure itself. New track was laid on heavy section plastic railbearers and the overhead was replaced in time for the start of the 2015 season. Removal of the Ballure scaffolding mountain took a little longer. The refurbishment cost over £1m but safeguarded the structure and the MER's approach to Ramsey for the next thirty years. To complement the 1899 plaque commemorating the original designer and contractor, a new plaque, of similar design, faces it, commemorating the involvement of The Department of Infrastructure, Auldyn Construction, Silva Primary Consulting, Burroughs Stewart Associates and Manx Rail Projects in 2015. Evidently modern maintenance and upgrading can be more complex than new design and construction. Auldyn Construction is a long established Manx contractor, although it is now part of the Colas group. Silva are consulting quantity surveyors and Burroughs Stewart are consulting engineers, both based in Douglas. Manx Rail Projects ceased operations around the end of 2016, but were based in Laxey.

WAITING SHELTERS

There is wide variety in the designs of the waiting shelters along the line. This springs from the past and present usage of the stops concerned, and, in some cases, the pressure exerted by the local populace and, inevitably, economics. Historically the wayside shelters were either built in wood or formed of corrugated iron, and provided basic weather protection from the frequent local rain and wind. In the past, when a winter service was operated, protection from snow was a real benefit. The ravages of time have taken their toll and many of the shelters on the Douglas to Laxey section of line have now been replaced by utilitarian steel and glass 'bus stop' structures similar to those found along the island's bus routes. The modern steel waiting shelters are manufactured by Macemain & Amstad of Corby, England, a UK manufacturer and supplier of contemporary structures and street furniture. The shelters are of modular design, enabling a variety of sizes to be constructed from the basic parts. The traditional shelters have generally survived on the Laxey to Ramsey section and are usually painted in MER green, although some brown preserved-wood structures have appeared. Replacements in this more rural area have, so far, avoided the steel and glass 'bus stop' designs which are becoming so prevalent in the Douglas to Laxey section.

Derby Castle

The facilities at Derby Castle are decidedly basic considering that it is one of the principal stations on the line and the terminus in the island's capital. Most island visitors will find their way here by heading north along the promenades, quite possibly on board a horse tram. There is none of the grandeur associated with the steam railway station at the other end of Douglas. This is an historic hangover: in late Victorian days the Isle of Man Tramways and Electric Power Company (IoMTEP) had bought the horse tramway and intended to extend electric working along the length of the promenades. The repercussions of the collapse of Dumbell's Bank in 1900 and the subsequent separation of the ownership of the horse and electric tramways, between Douglas Corporation and the Manx Electric Railway effectively wrecked that plan. The MER has been confined to the north end of the promenade ever since, and the promenade was served by the Douglas Corporation horse tramway. In 2016 ownership of the horse tramway was transferred to the Isle of Man Transport, when Douglas Corporation was no longer willing to continue funding its operation from the town's rates, so after an interval of well over 100 years

A view taken inside Ballure Viaduct during refurbishment, note the scaffolding and planking. Thanks are due to the resident engineer for a guided tour of the work in progress (28 February 2015)

Right: the combined bus and tram shelter at Derby Castle, complete with a matching pair of flags, stands behind tunnel car 9, with its original illuminations scheme (4 May 2003)

Below: for about two years, the body of former Lisbon tram 360 served as a waiting room at Derby Castle. Purchased by the MER in 1996, 360 was built in 1907 and last saw service in Lisbon in 1993 (5 May 2001)

the two lines are once again operated by the same body.

For a few years at the start of the twenty-first century a former Lisbon tram body was parked at Derby Castle and provided covered seating for waiting passengers: this replaced a rather less exotic pensioned off Leyland National bus, number 26 in the Isle of Man Transport fleet, which had been used in the late 1990s. The tram body is now in private ownership and resides in the garden of a dwelling in Ballasalla. It can be seen from the main A5 road near the roundabout leading to the Balthane Industrial Estate. The Leyland National bus survived until April 2016 when it finally succumbed to the scrap metal merchants.

Onchan Head

The site which lies to the seaward side of the line at Onchan Head was formerly occupied by the White City Pleasure Park, complete with all the fairground facilities and a roller-coaster that would be associated

Above: hardly a structure or shelter, but the seat which previously graced the Onchan Head stop carries a sign-written 'Manx Electric Railway' as well as a relaxed passenger (2 May 1999)

Left: a typical bus stop style shelter on the King Edward Road section of line near Douglas. This one is at Onchan Head. The prospective passenger seen in the previous photograph hails a tram. Even though she is wearing the same scarf, she has not been waiting that long (9 April 2015)

with such an attraction. Now replaced by late twentieth-century housing, with access from a road along the cliff tops beyond the houses, traffic demand has reduced substantially. In White City's heyday short-working cars would bring pleasure seekers here from Derby Castle and return downhill having used the crossover. Collecting fares from a full load on the short trip down the hill would have been too much of a challenge for even the most nimble conductor, so the facilities here included a ticket office, staffed in the holiday season, and a shelter. With the demise of the White City Pleasure Park the station buildings were demolished in 1978 and a simple bench, with no shelter, was deemed sufficient for the passenger demand. In the twenty-first century an (infrequent) bus service was introduced along King Edward Road and a 'bus stop' steel and glass shelter provided for passengers by either road or rail. Certainly a step up in the weather protection league from the exposed bench.

Majestic, Braeside and Far End

All three of these stops are provided with steel and glass 'bus stop' type shelters, practically identical to that at Onchan Head, and which also cater for bus passengers on the parallel route 13 bus services. Situated on the land side of the line adjacent to the access roads to the houses on the inland side of King Edward Road they provide basic, dry, accommodation.

Howstrake

Lying on the sea side of the line at the Howstrake summit are the remains of a substantial rendered-stone shelter adjacent to the access road leading down to the former Howstrake Holiday Camp. The shelter was built around 1910 by the camp and maintained by them until the camp closed in 1973. There are still remains of some of the camp buildings and its swimming pool lying between the tramline and the cliffs, although these are not readily visible from the tramway. Access to the camp was provided from both sides of the line and a walking route was available through the gateway on the inland side which led to a 'tunnel' beneath the tracks and King Edward Road to the camp itself (see page 31-2). Sadly the stone shelter has suffered from the ravages of time and the gentle falling away of the cliff has damaged the seaward side rear wall. At the time of writing the shelter is fenced off from public access on the road and tramway side to protect public safety. In the absence of holiday camp traffic there is little demand at this stop so it appears unlikely that a replacement structure will be provided. Passengers must wait on the exposed headland.

The massive shelter at Howstrake, built by the owners of the former holiday camp. Despite the camp having closed 45 years previously the legend 'Howstrake Holiday Camp Station' is still just legible at the top of the shelter. The 'Buy Me' sign relates to the Howstrake site - not the shelter! (7 October 2018)

Groudle Old Road

This stop, about mid-way between Howstrake and Groudle Glen, serves the nearby Groudle Holiday Cottages, which lie below the line. Many of these are now occupied throughout the year and the road through the estate provides access to the lower part of the glen, Groudle Beach and, by a path up to Lime Kiln Halt, the Groudle Glen Railway. A 'bus stop' steel and glass shelter, similar to that at Onchan Head, is provided on the landward side of the line. At the time of writing, passengers may also admire a very nice small garden recently laid out beside the shelter. Rumour has it that it was intended for the Groudle Glen stop, as part of the 125th anniversary of the tramway celebrations, but inadvertently placed a stop early. But they are only rumours.

Groudle Glen

This was the original, 1893, terminus of the line and the facilities here were designed as an adjunct to the commercial development of the glen. On the land side of the line a large wooden shelter is provided which is capable of holding around a hundred intending passengers – something which can easily happen when the nearby Groudle Glen Railway is operating. The building incorporates a ticket office at the Douglas end, aimed at reducing the demands on conductors' energies when crowds returned to their hotels in Douglas after concerts in the glen. The ticket office is now disused as current demand is insufficient. The shelter is a painted wooden structure, 47'-6" (14.5m) long by 12'-0" (3.7m) wide, nestles against the hill and has a truss roof supported on the outer edge by wooden pillars.

Right: the commodious shelter at Groudle Glen is impressive and well maintained. The former ticket office is at the far end of the building. Alongside the shelter is one of the post-boxes that were served by the MER collection service until 1975 (5 October 2013)

Below right: adjacent to the Groudle shelter is a commemorative plaque unveiled by the Lieutenant Governor, Air Marshal Sir Lawrence Jones, on the occasion of the tramway's centenary on 7 September 1993 (5 October 2013)

On the opposite side of the road from the tram station is the large building, designed by the architect Baillie Scott, which was formerly the Groudle Glen Hotel. It opened in 1893 as part of the development of the Howstrake Estate that the tramway was intended to serve. The entrance to the glen's pleasure grounds lies to the right of the hotel and paths lead down past a water wheel to the bandstand. With the decline in tourism the hotel was sold by the brewery in 1999 and transformed into a restaurant named 'La Casa'. This venture proved relatively short lived and this business closed a few years ago. At the time of writing the building is for sale but it seems unlikely that it will re-open as either a pub or restaurant. Planning permission has been sought to demolish the property and build houses on the site.

Halfway

The tramway joins the main coast road, the A2, at Halfway, called such as it is the tramway's mid-point between Douglas and Laxey. The stop is also known as Baldromma, after the nearby farm, or as Liverpool Arms after a neighbouring hostelry. Sadly the Liverpool Arms closed abruptly in October 2017 and, at the time of writing, planning permission has been granted for conversion to a six-bedroom residence. The Liverpool Arms' sudden closure annoyed the author as he had alighted from a tram for lunch and had a long wait for the next tram to an alternative establishment.

Halfway has a 'Request Stop' sign, which, unusually, does not give the stop's name, plus a post box set into an adjacent stone pillar.

Trackwork is under way during the closed season at Halfway with the shared bus and tram shelter on the right of the construction plant and the pile of new sleepers (25 January 2014)

Until 1975 the MER conductors were sworn in as auxiliary postmen and specified tram services cleared the mailboxes along the line, the trams being met by a post van at Derby Castle. On the road side of the tramway is a bus lay by: this is a further example of a dual-purpose facility as the steel and glass shelter between the tramway and the road also serves passengers using the frequent service provided by the route 3 and 3A buses on the main road, as well as the route 13 local buses. Shortly beyond the stop the MER crosses the main road at a light controlled crossing (see page 46).

Ballameanagh

Ballameanagh has increased in importance since a new substation (see page 15), constructed during 2017, has been providing power to the tramway. The steel and glass 'bus stop' shelter provided was relocated a short distance to the north of its previous position, and is now reached by a short concrete path outside the new substation's compound. Because of the changes the stop is now sometimes referred to as Barroose, after the farm on whose land the substation now stands.

Baldrine

The picturesque shelter at Baldrine typifies the classic appearance of an MER stop. The shelter is immaculate and composed of green-painted corrugated iron cladding on a timber frame, with an MER nameboard on the roof. The shelter was substantially rebuilt in 1991-2. Standing next to it is a post box in its own rendered stone pillar, similar to many that were situated along the line.

Ballagawne

Having detoured around Garwick Glen the MER rejoins the coast road at Ballagawne Road. On the inland side of the line a steel and glass 'bus stop' type shelter stands adjacent to the road crossing. On the opposite side of the road a similar shelter serves Douglas-bound buses, but the restricted sightlines mean that northbound bus users will not find the tram shelter convenient for their purposes. The sharp curve of the MER as it emerges from Garwick Glen means that most intending tram passengers will first be aware of their approaching service from the squeal of wheel on rail as their tram rounds the head of the Garwick Glen a quarter of a mile away.

Ballabeg

The tram stop lies shortly after the tramway crosses the second light-controlled level crossing on the route from Douglas. A footpath leads from the main road past houses to the stop. The wood-framed corrugated-iron structure, substantially rebuilt in 1992, is painted in standard MER green and has been adopted by some local residents, as it is surrounded by a number of potted plants and garden ornaments. The name is carried on a roof board. As is now standard

Left: Ballabeg shelter and the section box between the tracks are, like the shelter at Baldrine (see page 25), also well looked after by sympathetic local residents. Is there a friendly rivalry with their opposite numbers along the line? The ambiance is not assisted by a couple of old wire reels and piles of old sleepers dumped beyond the shelter. It is very early in the operating season, so perhaps the engineers will soon be tidying up (25 March 2016)

practice this comprises a plastic board with computer-generated text. Although clear and durable these new boards lack the distinctive character of the sign-written wooden boards they are replacing. The adjacent electrical section box has had its original IoMTEP lettering picked out and adds to the local colour.

Fairy Cottage

On the descent into Laxey, Fairy Cottage's shelter stands on the seaward side and is accessed from the nearby road via a short, steep footpath. This is also a wood-framed corrugated-iron structure, reconstructed in 1992, but now carries its nameboard on the side facing the tramway, rather than on the roof. Unlike the shelters at Baldrine and Ballabeg it lacks windows facing onto the tramway.

Above: Fairy Cottage's shelter is located on the seaward side of the line. It is hidden from the main road by a row of houses but finding the pathway between them is rewarding as the gardens here are well kept (22 June 2014)

Left: South Cape recently received new plastic signage. The previous signwritten wooden boards used a distinctive letter A, which is not perpetuated on the replacements. It is one of the very few shelters to be completely open fronted, and the only traditional green corrugated-iron clad shelter to be so (12 April 2015)

South Cape

The signage at South Cape has varied over the years. Before the 1970s it carried a subtext: 'Alight Here for The Beach'. In the modernized, upper and lower case lettering used when the tramway was branded as part of the Isle of Man Railways, this became 'Alight Here for Laxey Beach. Keep Your Seats for Laxey'. When traditional signwriting made a comeback, 'Keep Your Seats for Laxey' was lost. Since 2015 the basic 'South Cape' has been deemed sufficient on the modern plastic board. Laxey Beach is not far away, but it is a steep climb back up to the tram stop. The shelter is open on the tramway side and is another wood-framed, green-painted corrugated-iron structure and sits on the outside of the curve on the seaward side of the line. Unusually the stop can be accessed from two roads which cross the line with a path running parallel to the line.

Minorca

Uniquely for the MER the Minorca stop is situated above road level and is reached by a long flight of stone steps from Minorca Hill, which is spanned by the adjacent viaduct (see page 19). The steps form part of the abutment of the uphill side of the viaduct. The wood-framed, green-painted, corrugated-iron, waiting shelter is positioned at the top of the steps beside the northbound line. This structure was originally at Halfway, but it is unclear when it was relocated. It was thoroughly refurbished in 2015. A clear view across the Laxey valley to South Cape means that prospective passengers can normally see their next northbound tram about ten minutes before it arrives: the inland detour to Laxey and the dwell time there leading to the protracted wait. A small, tarmaced, waiting area serves southbound passengers at the top of the embankment.

Above: the shelter at Minorca received a major overhaul over the 2014-5 winter and looks resplendent, when this photograph was taken in the following spring. In a relatively exposed location, high above the Laxey valley, this shelter has an end doorway rather than one facing the track (29 March 2015)

Left: the waiting shelter is on the right at the top of this stairway from Minorca Hill. The steps are built against the abutment and approach from the uphill side, giving a shorter climb than would be the case from the far side (14 May 2012)

Dhoon Glen (and café)

The shelter at Dhoon Glen (see page 28) is built of wood treated in preservative and is a replacement erected in 1987. Situated on the inside of the curve it is adjacent to the Dhoon Glen café and the picnic spot at the head of the paths leading down the glen to the secluded beach, around 160 yards below. The café is a rendered stone or brick building, with conveniences located underneath and accessed by the steps adjacent to the shelter. The café is owned by the tramway but operates on a contract basis and is usually open when the trams are operating.

Glen Mona

Although the flourishing foliage here may suggest a relatively isolated spot, the Glen Mona stop is conveniently

Right: the shelter at Dhoon Glen accommodates seating and tables which may be used by the patrons of the adjoining café, which has no interior seating. In recent years block paving has improved the ambiance of this stop (4 October 2015)

Below: since the Glen Mona shelter was replaced, the undergrowth has flourished and the shelter is now almost engulfed. The post box used to be on the left but all traces have now gone (12 September 2015)

situated near the village and the Glen Mona Hotel, which lies a short distance above the stop along a footpath. A small shelter, once again built of treated wood, lies on the seaward side of the line and is a replacement constructed in 1988. Many of the shelters on the Laxey to Ramsey section were treated in this era: presumably rain and rot affected most of the original structures at the same time. Formerly there was a post box on a pillar on the Ramsey side of the shelter but this was removed following the cessation of postal collections by the MER at the end of the 1975 season.

Ballaglass

Unusually this stop and its shelter are remote from any road access. Ballaglass halt is at the head of the glen of the same name and can be reached by a network of footpaths which connect the main road with the sylvan delights of the glen. The MER used to own the glen, but, apart from charging an entry fee and selling refreshments, it remained uncommercialized. The

The gate was added to the Ballaglass shelter after the local wild goat population realised it was better inside than out in the rain. They were not a problem but their droppings were. Note the characteristic signwritten **A** *on the nameboard, a feature which is fast disappearing as new plastic boards appear (16 September 2015)*

shelter is once again a replacement structure, erected in 1989, of treated wood and is located under the trees. The two ends of the shelter feature unglazed pentagonal apertures. Oddly the shelter carries a nameboard proclaiming 'Ballaglass' but the flag on the adjacent traction pole is labelled 'Ballaglass Glen'.

Cornaa

The Cornaa stop lies on a hairpin bend in the tramway by a level crossing with a minor road which serves the local community and a former water mill. Usually the wooden shelters are treated with preservative, but Cornaa is painted in MER green, similar to the corrugated-iron structures, which it mimics. On the outside of the curve it affords a clear view of approaching trams from either direction.

Above: Cornaa shelter at the end of the operating season in 2013. The wooden, signwritten nameboard was replaced by a new-style plastic equivalent early in 2017 (2 November 2013)

Ballajora

Ballajora boasts one of the most capacious shelters on the country section of the tramway. A long shelter placed parallel to the land side line, it has a door at the Ramsey end. A window at the Laxey end provides views of approaching trams from a sheltered position and two more windows face the track. The shed is constructed of wood, with a corrugated iron cladding and painted in MER green. The adjacent post box is the last survivor of those on the Laxey to Ramsey section of line. During the early months of 2018 the shelter was substantially rebuilt as the wooden frame had decayed and collapse appeared imminent. A new concrete block retaining wall has been built behind and supports the wooden rear wall of the shelter and its cladding.

Above: the large shelter at Ballajora is seen from the rear of trailer 51, together with the sole surviving post box on the Laxey to Ramsey stretch of line; unusually the pillar has not received a coat of white paint. During periods of heavy rain the sandbags near the post box assist with directing the flow of water away from the access path and into the drain (29 July 2017)

Left: during the winter of 2017-8 Ballajora shelter received major attention and this work is shown underway, with temporary strengthening props in place. To provide access to the back wall the bench seat has been moved and reposes on the opposite side from its normal location. The shelter was ready for use by the start of the season (4 February 2018)

Dreemskerry

Down the hill towards Ramsey lies the Dreemskerry stop with its corrugated iron shelter built into the steep hill on the landward side of the line. Windows are provided facing the track and at the Laxey end. Providing the undergrowth is under control, a view of approaching trams is available, though intending passengers need to keep a sharp look out as descending trams arrive very shortly after turning the corner. The interior bench is believed to have been taken from tunnel car 5, which was converted to transverse seating as long ago as 1932. If this is true then, given the ingress of damp from the retaining wall, the continued existence of the bench is remarkable. The shelter is painted in MER green and, rather than a roof mounted nameboard, there is a free-standing board next to the shelter. Some local enthusiasts have provided a chair so that they may wait in comfort on nice days.

At the time of writing Dreemskerry retains its rather weatherworn signwritten name board. The shelter is unique in that it has a domestic style closing door. Occasionally local farmers move sheep along the line and it is not unknown for a tup to be temporarily incarcerated inside the shelter, the door secured by a bungee strap! (9 March 2017)

Lewaigue

At the end of the long downhill straight from Dreemskerry the next shelter is at Lewaigue, adjacent to the minor road crossing of Jack's Lane. A small replacement shelter, dating from the late 1980s, it is once again in treated wood with a roof-mounted nameboard and stands on the landward side of the line. Interestingly the original shelter that was here until superseded by the present one still survives. At the time of writing it is in the former goods yard at Laxey and has been restored to show what an original wayside MER shelter would have looked like.

Above: Lewaigue adjoins the nearby Venture Centre which occasionally charters special trams for its guests. This provides the rare occurrence of an MER trip not starting at one of the principal stations (14 April 2017)

Left: the original Lewaigue shelter plus a reconstructed post box pillar, as restored by the Laxey and Lonan Heritage Trust volunteers and located near the goods shed at Laxey. Van 16 is on an isolated piece of track (22 April 2018)

Bellevue

The final shelter on the northern section of the MER is at Bellevue adjoining the level crossing of the Ramsey to Maughold Road. The shelter dates from the early part of the twenty-first century. Local opinion resisted the proposed installation of a steel and glass 'bus stop' shelter. A more acceptable open-fronted treated wood structure stands on the land side of the line. Unusually the nameboard is a free-standing one on the opposite side of the tracks from the shelter. A post box was previously located between the road crossing and the shelter, but like most others on the northern section of the line, this was removed following the cessation of postal collections by tram.

Above: the open fronted shelter is of a type unique to the MER. Very few shelters include a water butt but those which do make it easier for volunteers to maintain the lineside display of flowers (16 May 2012)

Left: unusually the Bellevue board is on the opposite side of the line from the shelter. Winter saloon 21 and trailer 47 head south towards Douglas on a bank holiday weekend service (30 August 2015)

MISCELLANEOUS STRUCTURES

'Tunnel' access to Howstrake Holiday Camp

Near Howstrake summit, but on the way down towards Groudle Glen, there is a 'tunnel' passing below the road and the tramway. In engineering terms, this is not a tunnel but a bridge, as both road and tramway are carried on an embankment and the passageway beneath them was incorporated as part of the construction works. When the tramway opened, a recreational area, Howstrake Park, was developed, with paid entry through the gateway on the inside of the curve opposite the present Howstrake shelter. Tourists could enjoy the views from the paths on hillside both above and below the line, with the passageway connecting the two areas. The embankment carrying the tramway and its parallel road is approximately 15ft (5m), above the flat floor level of the tunnel, which has vertical stone sides and an arched masonry roof. The tunnel is approximately 10ft (3m) wide and 8ft (2.5m) high at its centre line. On the inland side of the line a set of steps, parallel with the line, leads down to the tunnel entrance from the gateway. Evidently the attractions of Groudle Glen were more popular than those of the Howstrake hillside as the latter was only open for a few years.

The seaward part of the park was soon incorporated into Cunningham's International Young Men's Holiday Camp which opened in 1897, some four years after the tramway. In 1907 this became known as the Howstrake Holiday Camp, which closed in 1973. The remains of the camp are largely invisible from the tramway, but a number of derelict buildings survive on the headland above Groudle Beach. Since closure, the undergrowth has thrived and very little is now visible of the tunnel which connected the camp to the path and the wrought iron gates opposite the Howstrake Camp shelter.

On the coast side of King Edward Road, away from the tramline, a low parapet lies above the point of emergence of the tunnel onto the camp site. This is shortly downhill from the set of steps which mark the site of the former camp entrance lodge facing onto the road.

Looking from the seaward side the tunnel below King Edward Road and the tramway at Howstrake Camp. Beyond tunnel the path climbs some stone steps towards the gateway at Howstrake summit. The structure is in good condition, although the floor has accumulated a deep layer of mud (11 May 2017)

As the tunnel dates from the opening of the first part of the MER in 1893 it is the oldest load-carrying structure on the line, predating the major masonry viaduct at Groudle Glen which opened to traffic in the following year. Supporting the weight of both rail and road traffic on King Edward Road the access tunnel is an historic artefact, but practically invisible to the vast majority of road and rail users.

Laxey Power Station off Glen Road

When the Manx Electric Railway was extended from Groudle Glen to Laxey in 1894 the power station at Derby Castle was too remote to supply power at the northern extremity of the line (see chapter 4). Accordingly, a new masonry power station was constructed in Laxey where a plentiful supply of boiler and cooling water was available from the Laxey River (see photograph on page 63). Laxey harbour was suitable for the import of coal for the furnaces, with haulage along Glen Road by horse-drawn cart. The Laxey valley has a certain susceptibility to flooding during extreme weather events and the presence of the river was to prove a mixed blessing.

The former power station situated below the tramway at Ballaglass. The accumulator house is on the left while the coal store, on the right, is now a swimming pool. The power plant was in the centre (16 September 2015)

The Laxey power station was decommissioned when the MER switched to transforming high tension AC from the island grid in the 1930s: the building survives in non-railway use.

Ballaglass Power Station

Ballaglass Power station (see lower photograph opposite) was constructed in stone to supply power to the northern half of the Manx Electric Railway, and was commissioned with the Laxey to Ballure section of line in 1898. Situated on the land side of the line on the Laxey side of Ballaglass Halt and Glen, the site was selected to use the water from the stream for steam generation and cooling. Coal was brought along the MER from Ramsey and delivered by gravity down the embankment.

Following the 1930s upgrade of the MER electricity supply to use the island's high tension AC grid, the power station was taken out of use and the generating plant removed. Thereafter overhead power was supplied from an on-site substation which survived until a new facility was brought into use at Ballagorry bridge in 1989, after which the Ballaglass buildings were sold. Structurally the main buildings have been remarkable survivors, although the chimney, which stood between the building and the embankment at the north end of the site, has been demolished. At the end of a long approach drive from the main Douglas to Ramsey road, the structure was converted into a private residence during the 1990s. Despite the proximity of the tramway the house does not have easy access to the tram stop and a walk down the drive and back along the footpath is necessary to reach Ballaglass Halt.

SNAEFELL MOUNTAIN RAILWAY

The Snaefell Mountain Railway has relatively few structures, but the majority have been replaced over the years. The original structures were constructed to meet immediate requirements for the line's opening, at a low cost and not to particularly high standards. Laxey Station is the junction with the MER and the facilities have already been described (see pages 5-7) as it caters for both lines.

Laxey Car Shed

The first car shed for the Snaefell Mountain Railway (SMR) was constructed in 1895 with two roads to hold the original fleet of six cars. It was adjacent to the original SMR station just above Laxey Village and on the site of the current shed. Extension of the running lines downhill to Dumbell's Row saw the car shed on a short branch line and this has remained the case ever since. The original shed comprised brick built walls supporting a corrugated iron roof arch. It was just sufficient to hold the operating fleet. Ancillary vehicles such as the tower wagon and open trucks were parked on sidings outside.

Above: the 1995 steel portal frame car shed for the Snaefell tram fleet at Laxey. The original Laxey terminus was on the left of this picture (9 June 2017)

Left: the shed which houses the NATS railcar is situated to the north side of the trackwork leading to the Snaefell car shed. One of the SMR four-wheeled maintenance trucks stands in front of the doors (9 June 2017)

Snaefell Car 6 is experiencing some problems beside King Edward Road, Onchan, on its way back from the workshops at Derby Castle to Laxey following a body overhaul. The Hopkinson bow collectors have been removed for this move; any interaction with the live MER overhead must be avoided. Two staff members are standing by while a third is attending to either the accommodation bogie or some other item beneath the car. (Courtesy Travel Lens Photographic, May 1986)

In the centenary year of the line, 1995, the original car shed at Laxey was replaced by a new steel portal frame structure with three roads, which created space for additional workshop facilities to handle overhauls and major maintenance activities. For many years the Snaefell car bodies were taken to the Derby Castle workshops for major overhauls and repairs: the bodies being switched to spare 3'-0" gauge trailer bogies on the mixed gauge siding in Laxey Station. Travel to and from Douglas saw the Snaefell cars being towed along the Manx Electric Railway. After 1995, the mixed gauge siding in Laxey station was no longer used for transferring the bodies. Interestingly, when the trackwork at Laxey Station was replaced over the winter of 2013-4, the Snaefell siding nearer the MER was re-laid with mixed gauge track. However as there is no physical connexion to the MER, the 3'-0" gauge rails cannot be used.

In the post-war years National Air Traffic Services (NATS) opened a radio station on the summit of Snaefell to assist in the control of flights over the Eastern Atlantic Ocean. In order to provide year-round access to the facilities it has operated a variety of internal combustion Wickham railcars which can reach the summit even when the electric power is switched off. A small brickwork shed on the northern part of the Snaefell depot site houses the railcar when not in use.

The NATS Wickham railcar received a major overhaul off island in early 2018. Looking resplendent outside the shed the newly refurbished unit waits its next call to duty (2 April 2018)

Power station

The remains of the Snaefell power station and one of the boilers may be seen below the line in the Laxey valley shortly below The Bungalow station. Using local materials it was built of stone with a slate roof (see chapter 4).

Bungalow station

When the line opened in 1895 a basic shelter was provided where the line crosses the mountain road. The popularity of the mountain railway justified an upgrade in facilities, and the following year the Bungalow Hotel was opened. This was a gabled wooden structure on the south side of the line above the mountain road which provided refreshment facilities. The Bungalow later served as the transfer point to a charabanc service which provided connexions to the 'Manx Switzerland', otherwise known as the Sulby Valley. After visiting the tea rooms at Tholt-y-Will, onward travel led to the Manx Northern Railway line at Sulby enabling tourists to complete a round trip by tram, coach and steam train. The Bungalow Hotel served until it was demolished in 1958 following structural deterioration. The facilities here were reduced once more to a basic ticket office and waiting shelter, which had the appearance of an adapted wooden garden shed.

Above: the roof lettering is reminiscent of Laxey Station and leaves no doubt about the building's identity. The wooden chalet is in excellent condition and presents a welcoming facade to passing trade on the mountain road. The tramway crosses the road to the right of the photograph with the station facilities on the far side of the hotel (Courtesy Travel Lens Photographic 1920s)

Left: an ascending car has halted at The Bungalow in May 1956, when the hotel was looking past its best. This view is looking down from the footpath to the summit and the tramway spirals round behind the photographer. There is no footbridge over the TT course as yet (R. B. Parr, Courtesy Travel Lens Photographic 20 May 1956)

Right: the passenger facilities at Bungalow were minimal following the demolition of the original building in 1958 until the construction of the present station in 2002. Note that only one mast graces the summit (1970s commercial postcard)

The current Bungalow station building seen from Snaefell, together with the footbridge spanning the TT Mountain Course. Behind and to the right of the station is the workyard for the reconstruction works following the storms of 2015 (see chapter 3) (23 April 2016)

The modernization of the railways' power supply extended to the Snaefell line in 2002 and this saw the replacement of the substation located in the buildings of the former power station. Modern, solid state, substation facilities were incorporated into the building, which also provided a station master's office, ticket office, waiting room and toilets in a structure far superior to the basic wooden hut that it superseded. No public refreshment facilities are provided from this building, although the adjacent car park hosts fast food vans to satisfy the needs of spectators during the TT and Manx Grand Prix events when the Mountain Course is home to motorcycle racing. During road closures for the races the tram service does not cross the road but operates two independent shuttle services from Laxey and the summit.

Summit Hotel

The summit originally hosted a single-storey station building which was situated a short distance away from the single-storey hotel reached by a duckboarded walkway. The hotel facilities at the summit proved popular, so they were enhanced for the 1896 season at the same time as the construction of The Bungalow Hotel.

The original Summit Hotel was destroyed by fire on the night of 5-6 August 1982. Getting fire engines to the summit presents difficulties and the delay meant that the structure was completely gutted. The current building was erected during 1983 and opened for the 1984 season. Bringing construction material and personnel to the summit was facilitated by adding a siding at the Bungalow to handle the transhipment of men and equipment between road and rail.

The 1983 building survives in use today and has been refurbished to a high standard to provide welcome shelter and refreshment facilities. All supplies and staff are brought to the summit by the SMR, with a staff car leaving Laxey in advance of the public service. Mains electricity is available and water is drawn from a private well.

Car 2 is parked by the Summit Hotel, where roof maintenance is taking place. Even though the building takes advantage of what little cover there is on Snaefell, winter storms batter the structure and essential repairs are a feature of the summer season. The flag shows that a strong breeze is blowing today (19 July 2016)

CHAPTER 2

PERMANENT WAY

The initial installation on the MER used flat-bottom rails, often called Vignoles' rails after the engineer who introduced this cross-section to Europe; these were directly spiked to creosoted wooden sleepers. Such a form of construction was inexpensive and simple to lay, with relatively few components which were easily handled by manual labour in the Victorian era. The resulting trackwork was lighter and cheaper than that used on the mainline railways in the UK, which had standardized on heavy cast-iron chairs supporting bullhead rail. Although bullhead rail gave a more robust track capable of sustaining higher axle loads and speeds, this was achieved at a greater expense with more components per mile. The lighter vehicles of the MER, coupled with the lower speeds on the tramway, permitted such economies to be made. Rails were typically 56lb/yd (27.8kg/m) on the Douglas to Laxey section with 62.5lb/yd (31kg/m) on the later Laxey to Ramsey extension. This compares with typical main line standard bull-headed rails of 95lb/yd (47.1kg/m).

The principal exception to the standard trackwork on the MER was alongside Walpole Road in Ramsey which was laid with street tramway girder rail rolled in Belgium, and which came with a groove and check rail included. The original intention of the Ramsey Town Commissioners was that Walpole Road would be paved across its entire width and thus provide the MER with its only

Above: plain line near Dhoon Farm showing the traditional wooden sleepers with flat bottom rail secured directly by dog spikes (2 February 2014)

Left: Walpole Road in suburban Ramsey showing the present arrangement with plain track which superseded the original grooved rails. This is the nearest that the MER comes to running on street (13 July 2016)

section of street running tramway. The pair of tracks would have been running along the inland side of the highway rather than either side of the centre line. Normal practice for street tramways requires minimum clearances to be maintained between the pavement kerb and the nearest rail, leading to the tracks being in the centre of the road. In order to facilitate the free movement of street traffic, this section was equipped with long bracket arms supported by traction poles on the inland side, so that there would be no impediment to highway traffic from poles positioned between the tracks. Paving the full width of the street did not take place and, when the rails wore out in the late twentieth century, they were replaced with standard flat-bottom rail spiked to wooden sleepers. Walpole Road remains an otherwise quiet suburban street: full-width paving was never needed for the traffic levels.

During the twentieth century the renewal of worn track was generally carried out on a like-for-like basis. The 1950s replacement rail was to British Standard BS11 using 60lb/yd (29.8kg/m) flat-bottom material. The first edition of BS11 was issued in 1903: rails supplied before this date were to individual manufacturers specifications. The majority of the line still consists of flat-bottom rail directly spiked to treated wooden sleepers.

In the twenty-first century the MER modernized its approach to track renewals and a variety of changes have taken place as individual line lengths are replaced. An early occurrence was the replacement of the crossover at Fairy Cottage around 2009, which was re-laid with steel baseplates between the flat bottom rail and the sleepers with Pandrol rail clip fasteners. Pandrol clips had first become commonplace on UK mainline track in the 1960s so the Manx Electric Railway was approximately fifty years behind British Railways' practice. This was not the first island installation of Pandrol clips as the 2'-0" (610mm) gauge Groudle Glen Railway had used them when relaying some of its line a few years before this date. The addition of baseplates and Pandrol clips increases the initial cost of the track, but the wider spread of load on the sleeper reduces the cutting force of the edge of the rail foot and hence extends sleeper life with an overall cost saving.

An early application of Pandrol sprung rail clips on the MER. The recently relaid crossover at Fairy Cottage is seen with the engineers' markings. 'Site 39 Fairy Cottage, Crossover 5' and an arrow pointing towards Douglas guided the permanent way team during installation (18 May 2009)

Later installations have seen lengths of line re-laid with concrete sleepers and continuously-welded rail. An early instance was the otherwise routine replacement of the southbound line climbing from Groudle Glen towards Howstrake in about 2013. The pre-stressed concrete sleepers are cast specifically for the Isle of Man Railways (and identified as such from the moulds used) as there is relatively small demand for 3'-0" (914mm) gauge installations elsewhere in the British Isles. The connexion of the continuous welded rail to the standard (jointed) track is made through expansion (or 'breather') switches. For a long length of welded rail the friction forces which hold the rail in place need a considerable length to build up to full capacity through the individual rail fasteners. Although the bulk of the rail remote from the end sections is held immovable, under thermal expansion and contraction loads the relative movement at the ends of the welded lengths is far larger than that occurring at the ends of standard length jointed rails. The expansion switches provide smooth rail running surfaces at the ends of the section. Colloquially, they allow the rail to breathe, hence the alternative name of the switches. The sleepers supporting the breather switches are reinforced by affixing lengths of

Top left: concrete sleepers made their appearance on the MER during 2013. This sleeper end shows the moulded-in owner's identity: 'Isle of Man Railways' (5 October 2013)

Bottom left: a later sleeper showing it was supplied by Leonhard Moll, a manufacturer of prestressed concrete sleepers since 1937. Although a German company it has plants in Poland, the UK, the Czech Republic and Croatia. This sleeper is installed beside King Edward Road, near Howe Road in Onchan (2 April 2017)

A pair of breather, or expansion, switches installed at the end of a welded length of rail near Groudle Glen (5 October 2013)

channel sections bolted to four sleepers outside the running rails, which provide lateral strength and stability to the track. This compensates for the reduced lateral stiffness due to the lack of bending continuity in the rails at the switches.

Lubrication of the special baseplates supporting the expansion switches is a maintenance task that has been added to the routine upkeep of the line. In compensation, as the rails are welded, fishplated rail joints are absent and, as the rail welds provide full electrical connectivity, the tasks of checking fishplate bolt tightness and electrical continuity bonds have both been eliminated on the new sections of track. There is also no need to carry out routine removal and lubrication of fishplates.

When welded rails are installed, the individual rail lengths, with measured gaps between them, are fitted on site and the Thermite welding process is used to create the site welds. A crucible containing a mixture of ferrous oxide and aluminium is ignited generating a large amount of heat in an exothermic chemical reaction, which reduces the ferrous oxide to iron while oxidizing the aluminium. Molten iron is produced and fed into a mould embracing the rail head, web and foot, thus welding the two rail ends together. Surplus weld metal is subsequently ground off the rail to leave a smooth running surface. Typically, the reagents for a rail joint are supplied in a portable single-use container. The Thermite process was developed by the German chemist Hans Goldschmidt in 1893 (coincidentally the same year as the tramway opened to Groudle) and was first used for welding tram tracks in the German city of Essen in 1899. The tramway in Essen opened on 23 August 1893, a mere fifteen days before the public opening of the tramway between Derby Castle and Groudle Glen.

A site-welded rail joint on a grooved tramway rail section installed near Howe Road, Onchan, in early 2018 (8 March 2018)

Ideally track welding should be carried out when the rails are close to the average temperature they will experience in service. This reduces the effects of thermal stresses: on cold days the rails attempt to shrink and will go into tension. Excessive tension stresses may lead to weld failure if defects are present. Conversely, on hot days compressive stresses will be generated which can induce overall track buckling. The climate of the Isle of Man is such that the temperature range over the year is relatively small, which reduces the probability of failure from these effects.

In normal UK railway practice, rails are shop welded and conveyed to site on a train of bogie bolster wagons, the high lateral flexibility of the rails allowing them to follow any curves *en route*. This is not practical on the Isle of Man Railways, as maintaining both a welding plant and a train for use a few times a year would be uneconomical. In addition, the curves on the MER are much sharper than those on standard gauge main lines and the rails would be unable to flex sufficiently on the way to site. Shop welding in a controlled (i.e., warm and dry) environment is preferred as higher-quality joints can be produced. However this is also not practical on the MER so site welding is necessary.

In addition to the concrete sleepered sections, some parts of the line have been re-laid with wooden sleepers with baseplated track and Pandrol fixings, so recent years have seen a diversification away from the traditional sight (and sounds) of the MER track. From the maintenance point of view, a wider range of spares needs to be carried, but the newer track forms require less day to day attention. The longer expected life of concrete sleepers offsets their greater initial cost. Worn rails can normally be replaced on a like for like basis in due course, reducing both future material and manpower costs, as concrete sleepers can usually be left *in situ*.

Pandrol rail clips with steel baseplates on a new section of track at South Cape. This still uses the traditional fishplated joints. The wire with bolted connectors to the rail ends maintains the electrical continuity for the return current (26 March 2017)

When the station at Laxey was remodelled over the winter of 2013-4, grooved girder rail made a comeback on the MER, the previous use being the track in Walpole Road, Ramsey, (see page 37). A quantity of surplus rail was acquired from the cancelled Liverpool tram scheme at a very economical price. This heavy-duty rail section is far stiffer than the standard flat-bottom rail used elsewhere on the MER, indeed it is ideal for an intensive service of heavier vehicles. The Snaefell line and sidings in the station were also re-laid at the same time. Interestingly, the previous dual-gauge siding where the Snaefell cars could be transferred to the MER (with a swap of bogies) for work to be carried out at Derby Castle depot was also re-laid, although in the absence of pointwork there is no means for a MER car to access this third rail (see also page 34). Rather surprisingly, the Laxey relaying work used wooden sleepers, covered by a layer of stone chippings. As the top layer is permeable there would appear to be potential for the sleepers to rot: being buried they are not easily inspectable and it will be interesting to see how durable this arrangement is. Using concrete sleepers in this environment would appear to have been a more economic and less disruptive solution in the long term.

During the spring 2017 relay of track in the Howe Road area in Onchan, further supplies of Liverpool grooved girder rail were installed. Interestingly, the track alternates between using grooved rail on the straight and larger radius sections of line, while the smaller radius curves are laid in standard flat bottom rail. The girder rail has a high lateral bending stiffness and it is not practical to bend the rail to the smaller radii. The connexions between the grooved girder and flat bottom rails have required the production of special fabricated rail connectors which accommodate the difference between the depths of the two sections and provide a stiff connexion. A massive baseplate is bolted to two sleepers and stiffeners welded to the baseplate hold what would be the two different fishplate sections to the rail

Above: Laxey station was host to a mixed gauge siding accessible by either Snaefell or MER cars. Despite the crossing there is a single switch blade on the left hand rail - rolling stock must follow the right hand rail according to its gauge (16 May 2012)

Right: the new grooved rail of the mixed gauge siding. There is now no connexion to the MER, so only Snaefell cars can access this track (11 April 2014)

Work in progress in Laxey Station during the winter closure of 2013-4. New grooved tram rail fixed to wooden sleepers by Pandrol clips supported on baseplates is being installed. A liberal application of stone chips has now hidden the trackform from view (25 January 2014)

webs. Checking this complex connexion piece for weld defects must be an interesting challenge in the workshops and even more difficult once installed. The weld geometry introduces stress raisers, and the potential for fatigue under service loads cannot be ignored.

Over the winter of 2017-8 further relaying work was carried out on the line between Far End and Howstrake, in a similar form to that in the Howe Road area nearer to Douglas. Concrete sleepers and welded rails also appeared on the northern section of the MER when part of the land-side line was re-laid between Lewaigue and Bellevue stops during the summer of 2017. Further lengths were re-laid during 2018 between Dhoon Quarry and Glen Mona. More track is likely to be re-laid in this fashion, but the transition to continuous-welded rail over the whole line will take a long time; the traditional sound of trams running on jointed track will be with us for many years to come.

There are also a number of instances where heavier than normal flat bottom rails have been used. The level crossing at Ballagawne, near Garwick Glen, was re-laid in 2014-5. It appears to have been laid using heavy rail technology as a standard item supplied by Rosehill Rail, but adapted to the narrow gauge of the tramway by amending dimensions as necessary. Rosehill Rail is a UK company specializing in producing level crossings with wear-resistant rubber road surface panels which have

Above: the fishplates joining the grooved tramway rail sections are these stiff six-bolted items seen near Howe Road, Onchan (8 March 2018)

Right: the complex fitment, with a steel plate spanning two sleepers, connects the stiff section of the grooved tramway rail to the lighter and shallower flat-bottomed rail traditionally used by the MER. There is no direct web-to-web connexion. The complexity may lead to fatigue problems (8 March 2018)

Above: the rails on the level crossing appear to be standard heavy rail sections, hence the need for special adapter fishplates to join to the lighter MER rail sections either side of the crossing. The appearance suggests that two halves of standard fishplates have been welded together, but this arrangement will lead to stress raisers with poor fatigue life (5 April 2015)

Right: the level crossing at Ballagawne Road was replaced during the winter of 2014-5. The non-slip rubber panels can be renewed, making maintenance quick and very straightforward (5 April 2015)

been widely installed on UK railways. A number of other MER crossings have since been replaced using the Rosehill system. Special fishplate connexions to accommodate the disparate rail sections are needed either side of the crossing. The rails in the third (2009) car shed at Laxey also appear to be heavier than normal, being joined to standard rails outside the shed.

Adjacent to Laxey car shed the crossover was renewed during the early part of 2018. The new trackwork was installed one pole closer to Douglas than the original. As the new crossover was installed prior to removing the old there was a short interval where both were in place (see photograph below).

Point and crossing work is relatively expensive and special track items are always given detailed consideration. One unusual item of trackwork is the pair of tandem (three-way) points used to access the car sheds at Derby Castle, where

The new crossover is almost complete and the permanent way staff, Wickham railcar with trailer, bags of ballast and tools are in attendance. The crossover which is shortly to be removed is nearer the camera. In the background, car 26 and an open wagon are sheeted over on the Laxey car shed headshunt while car 30 stands under wraps outside the shed. As well as these three items of rolling stock the Wickham also spent much of the winter stored here under the covers (31 January 2018)

Clearance tests are carried out on the new crossover to the north of Laxey Station. A Simplex diesel is slowly manoeuvring tunnel car 6 with its trolley tied down and the power off. In the background the SMR track is visible (18 April 2014)

the restricted space justifies the additional cost and complexity (see page 9). More recently, the crossover installed in 2014 at Dumbell's Row, just outside Laxey Station, has required the design and fabrication of pointwork to fit on a relatively sharp curve: almost all other MER crossovers are installed in sections of straight line. Crossovers between parallel lines using a matching pair of standard turnouts require no special work and are thus the most economical. The crossovers at Derby Castle Station and at Ramsey Plaza Station are not quite straight but are of considerable antiquity. If they need replacement then local redesign of the trackwork could well be considered.

When the car shed at Ramsey was removed during the winter of 2016-7 redundant trackwork was also removed. As well as

Above: looking from Parsonage Road the old trackwork at Ramsey Station shows the site of the goods shed and the remains of its siding to the left, the storage siding used on busy days (e.g., during TT week) and the stub end of the main line. Unusually, the traction poles in Ramsey Station are painted red, as opposed to the standard green. The cars on the right are parked on the site of the Plaza Cinema (8 November 2018)

Right: the switches have been removed from the southbound line outside Ramsey Station and plain line, with Pandrol clips, is being installed. The shed will soon follow the switches (24 November 2016)

the rails that formed the headshunt and those inside the shed, the facing connexion from the southbound line was replaced with plain line incorporating a short length of new track secured with Pandrol rail clips.

Sharp curves see the application of check rails which bear on the rear of the wheel flanges on the inside of the curve so that the lateral forces due to centrifugal loads are shared between both wheels on each axle and hence reduce the tendency of the outer wheels to climb the rail. Check rails are a common sight along the line due to its sinuous nature.

On the Ballure Viaduct additional guard rails are placed outside and above the level of the running rails to help restrain a derailed tram from falling into Ballure Glen. Unusually, the guard rails are formed of Snaefell Mountain Railway double-headed Fell rail mounted in the horizontal plane by using special retaining chairs. The tracks across Ballure Viaduct are laid on waybeams, i.e., longitudinal members, which pass the vertical loads from the trams directly onto the bridge girders, rather than onto transverse sleepers. When the viaduct was refurbished over the winter of 2014-5 new waybeams were provided in synthetic plastic polymer material, probably polypropylene, coloured to look like wood. This appears to be a case of a full-size railway imitating what has been common practice on model railways for many years. Before the refurbishment, creosoted wood waybeams had been used here, but the replacement material will not rot and hence should have an extended lifespan.

The effect of bright sunlight on dark rails is to cause their temperature to rise, often to a surprising level above ambient temperature. The rails try to expand and any longitudinal restraint can induce high compressive rail stresses. Although the Isle of Man rarely sees very high temperatures, any longitudinal restriction of this expansion will cause compressive forces to develop in the rails, which could lead to lateral buckling of the track. Such buckling can be countered by providing supplementary lateral restraint to the rails: one location where this has been implemented is near Ballameanagh (see photograph right). A simple but very effective approach is to paint the webs and feet of the rails in known problem areas white: white reflects

Above: on sharp curves the running lines are fitted with check rails on the inside rail. These are at the south end of Walpole Road. Car 20 and trailer 41 head south (16 September 2015)

Right: work is in progress installing new running and guard rails on Ballure Viaduct following its major refurbishment over the 2014-5 winter. The guard rails are Fell rails, as used for braking purposes on the Snaefell Mountain Railway, and special fixtures hold them in place (21 March 2015)

Additional timbering is employed on this curve near Ballameanagh to resist any outward lateral buckling movement. While this spot is subject to direct sunlight the rail feet and webs have not received the white paint treatment (27 March 2017)

Left: near Ballaskeig, between Cornaa and Ballajora, the webs and feet of the northbound track have been painted white to reduce the effects of solar irradiation. Presumably this is not a problem on the southbound track (3 June 2018)

Below: one of the electronic wheel sensors installed at the Ballure level crossing early in 2015. There is no physical contact between the wheel flange and the sensor (28 January 2019)

solar irradiation, reducing the rails' temperature rise and hence the risk of track buckling. Revisiting the critical zones with fresh paint in the early part of the operating season is necessary to keep the risk low.

The MER has three light-controlled level crossings with the main A2 Douglas to Ramsey road, all of which have poor sightlines between road and rail users. The crossings are at Halfway (Baldromma), Ballabeg and Ballure.

In conjunction with the refurbishment of the Ballure viaduct over the winter of 2014-5 the tracks were relaid over the bridge and the adjacent level crossing. Simultaneously the light controls at Ballure were updated with electronic flange detectors on both tracks on both sides of the crossing. These detect an approaching or departing tram on either track, from either direction. When a tram nears the crossing, the flange detectors will activate both the road traffic lights, which are a pair of alternately flashing red lights mounted vertically, plus a steady white light which shows the motorman that the road traffic lights are activated. The detectors on the departure side cancel the signals.

On the crossings at Halfway and Ballabeg activation and cancellation of the signals are by treadles. This scheme was also used at Ballure until the end of the 2014 season. In normal use an approaching tram car will activate the crossing lights automatically as its wheel flanges run over a treadle. As with the Ballure crossing, the road traffic lights are a pair of flashing red stop lights – unlike at Ballure these are mounted horizontally – and a white light is shown to the motorman. On the departure side of the crossing a second treadle switches off both the traffic lights and the white lights. The conductor should check from the rear of the tram that the lights have been reset for road users.

If a tram is running wrong line over the treadle-controlled crossings, for instance when single-line working is in operation,

One of the wheel-flange-actuated treadles at the approach to the Halfway crossing. The wheel flange depresses the lever which switches on the traffic lights. If wrong line working is in operation this will not cancel the lights, even though the tram is travelling away from the level crossing (31 January 2019)

When the tram has passed a sensor at Ballure and triggered the traffic lights to display a stop signal to road users, this unit will show a confirmatory white light to the motorman of the tram. If no light is shown then the conductor will descend and guard the crossing with a red flag (28 January 2019)

Right: situated a short distance further away from the level crossing this push button switch stands between the tracks. It is easily accessible from the cab side window of a tram. If the traffic lights have not been cancelled when wrong line working is taking place then a brief halt to press the button will do the trick (31 January 2019)

Left: at Halfway car 20 and trailer 47 have actuated the traffic control lights and swing across the A2 coast road. The red lights flash alternately with an overlap to ensure that a red is always showing, as seen here (Sara Goodwins, 14 June 2015)

then the treadle arrangement will not work correctly, as the tram encounters the cancellation treadle before the activator. Manual press buttons are positioned either side of the crossings so that platform staff may trigger or cancel the lights as required. Any defect with the system requires a reversion to tried and tested Victorian technology – the conductor descends from the tram and guards the crossing with the red flag carried on all cars. Apart from these three special installations there are no signals on the MER and operation is on a line of sight basis.

Although the MER has adopted modern practices for track installation it adheres to traditional practices for maintaining the track geometry. Current practice on most railways is to employ on-track ballast-tamping machines to pack the stones below the sleepers in order to provide the required smooth 'top' and, on curves, cross-levels for comfortable running at speed. On-track tamping machines are expensive and the acquisition of a narrow gauge version that would only be lightly used is presumably hard to justify. The bulk of the MER and Snaefell Mountain Railway foundations lie on fairly solid rock, which is a permanent-way engineer's dream. The conjunction of low traffic speeds and light vehicles causes few problems with the substrate and hence maintenance is relatively straightforward. Therefore track packing and alignment are still largely carried out manually, although power tools are deployed where appropriate.

The installation of new track and a crossover near Mines Road, Laxey. The track has been jacked up to the required level and a selection of power tampers is visible in the foreground (26 March 2014)

SNAEFELL MOUNTAIN RAILWAY

The Snaefell Mountain Railway permanent way follows similar engineering principles to those of the Manx Electric Railway. The major difference is, of course, the provision of the supplementary Fell rail along the majority of the line. The Fell Incline Railway System was developed by the nineteenth-century engineer John Barraclough Fell as a means of permitting railway operation on far steeper lines than would be practicable under normal, i.e., pure adhesion conditions. A line which climbed the Isle of Man's only mountain needed something out of the ordinary to cope with the necessarily steep gradients. In order to accommodate the Fell rail, and the associated braking system on the cars, the track gauge is 3'-6" (1067mm) being 6" (153mm) wider than that of the Manx Electric Railway. The break of gauge at Laxey Station precludes through running and all passengers travelling to, or returning from, Snaefell must change cars at Laxey.

A typical section of mountain track near Laxey. The rails are secured via Pandrol clips on baseplates, while the double-headed Fell rail is supported on brackets secured to every sleeper (16 July 2017)

At the time of writing, the running lines of the SMR comprise jointed rails laid on wooden sleepers throughout. Continuous welded rail and concrete sleepers have yet to make their appearance. The original trackwork comprised Vignoles' (flat-bottom) rails directly spiked to creosoted wooden sleepers. Later renewals have seen many lengths of track re-laid with baseplates and Pandrol spring clip fixings, although wooden sleepers have continued to be used. This is similar to many sections of the Manx Electric Railway.

The centre line of the 65lb/yd (32kg/m) Fell rail is set to be 3.5 inches (89mm) above the top surface of the running rails so that the suspended brake gear on the cars does not foul the running lines when passing through points and crossings and clears the road surfaces at the two level crossings. The double-headed Fell rail is mounted horizontally, i.e., the rail web is horizontal. As the surface level of the running rails will wear under traffic, and the bogie frames may settle on their springs under load, there needs to be tolerance in the Fell rail's exact height. Individual fastening brackets, formed out of folded sheet steel, are bolted to almost every sleeper to hold the Fell rails at the correct height. The Fell rail is fixed to the brackets and hence the sleepers by bolting through the Fell rail web. The inner ends of the cars' bogies have flanged wheels which lie on either side of the rail with a flange which lies below the rail so providing a degree of restraint against overturning. The wind forces on the exposed upper reaches of the line can be significant and operation of the line is suspended if the wind speed is predicted to become excessive. In each cab the Fell rail brake is actuated by a hand wheel which multiplies the force through a screw operated clamp onto the sides of the rail. Nowadays the Fell rail brakes are normally used for emergency braking only, but when the line was opened in 1895 they were the main brakes. Replacement of cast iron brake blocks was a regular occurrence as wear on the long descent took its toll. On some Fell railways the centre rail had been used to provide additional traction for ascending trains, with horizontally mounted driving wheels forced onto the rail sides, but this has never been employed on the Snaefell line where all traction forces are provided through adhesion.

There has only been one accident on the Snaefell Mountain Railway when a tram has catastrophically run away. Car 3 was parked just below the summit on the downhill line on 30 March 2016. For some reason, such as the brakes not being adequately secured, the tram started its journey downhill with neither crew nor passengers on board and naturally attained a considerable speed. It derailed on a bend above The Bungalow and the bodywork was totally destroyed. Fortunately there were no deaths or injuries. Enhanced braking systems were provided for the Snaefell cars and fitted during 2018, with the full fleet scheduled to be equipped for the start of the 2019 operating season.

The Fell rails are tapered at their ends to ease the take up of the brake clamps. The details may vary but this one near Laxey is typical (7 October 2018)

The Fell rail is not continuous throughout the line and there are relatively short lengths where it is not fitted. These include the station areas, the

Car 6 descends into Laxey having passed the green signal on the centre pole, showing that the single line section into Laxey Station is clear. Note that the mountain line is right hand running (16 July 2017)

road crossings at Laxey and The Bungalow and through any switch and crossing work. The tracks in and leading to the car shed a short distance uphill from Laxey, are practically level and again Fell rails are not fitted here. As the Fell rail is provided to augment the braking capacity of the cars on steep sections of the line the localized omission of the auxiliary braking facility on almost level sections does not create any safety difficulties.

Care is needed by the motormen and conductors to ensure that the jaws of the Fell rail brakes are wide open when the cars move onto a Fell rail section as otherwise the brake gear could be damaged by hitting it. The ends of the Fell rail are tapered to ease the pick up of the brake gear by the cars, which is carried out at low speed.

When originally opened, the Snaefell line station in Laxey was adjacent to the site of the current Snaefell car shed. The second station for the Snaefell line replaced the original when the line was projected downhill to terminate adjacent to the Laxey New Road, close to the current level crossing, but on the inland side. Finally, when the Manx Electric Railway was extended to Ramsey in 1898-9, the Snaefell line was extended once again across the New Road to share the current joint station. Prior to the opening of the Ramsey extension, the MER had terminated near the site of the current MER car sheds on the Douglas side of Glen Roy. Intending Snaefell passengers had to make their way by foot between the MER and SMR stations.

In order to provide continuity of the Fell rail for descending service cars, the first extension required the installation of a complex switch arrangement to provide access to the depot (see page 51-2). The second station, by Dumbell's Row, saw the line terminating in a stub with a single blade point, similar to that still provided at the summit, connecting the two running lines. The final extension to the current Laxey Station crosses Laxey New Road by a level crossing on a short stretch of single line, paralleling the twin tracks of the MER. The single line is controlled by colour light signals operated by the Laxey Station Master.

During the winter of 2017-8, a new signal was added to control the emergence of cars from the depot road as this movement involves a tram entering service travelling uphill towards descending service cars: the signal controls such conflicting movements. Cars returning to the depot from Laxey at the end of their duties need to travel on the wrong line and reverse above the depot pointwork.

In the late 1970s the Fell braking system was superseded by rheostatic braking in normal use (see page 72). Fell rail is not a standard section produced by steel rolling mills and is only supplied by special order. The original 1895 Fell rails needed replacement by the mid-1960s and in 1967 the MER funded a set of new rollers for the Workington steel mill to produce a batch of rail. The Snaefell line is the only line in the world still using the Fell rail system, so the lack of demand from other systems means there are no cost savings to be made by sharing an order. To obtain an economical price a significant length needs to be ordered to justify setting up the rolling mill to produce a batch of rail. There is currently a substantial stock of unused Fell rail stored in the yard by Dhoon Quarry on the MER line, from which stocks are drawn as required.

Installation of the Fell rail is not without its difficulties. As it is laid with the web horizontal, then any curves in the track require the Fell rail to be bent about its stiffer

The depot exit signal for Snaefell cars installed over the winter of 2017-8 and fitted to the final traction pole before the point. Note the adjacent stub of an old pole (7 January 2018)

Right: a supply of Fell rail supports at the Dhoon Quarry storage site. Although most have two bolt holes at the top there is a single bolt hole variant on the top of the second row from the right (7 January 2018)

Below: also at Dhoon is this stack of Fell rails. Fell is similar to bull-head rail, but has two identical heads as in use it will suffer wear on both surfaces, rather than the top wear that takes place on a running rail (7 January 2018)

major axis, whereas the running rails are bent about their more flexible minor axes. In some locations the geometric discontinuity of the Fell rail on sharp curves is quite noticeable. The Fell rails are fishplated in a similar manner to all other rail joints.

A feature of special interest is the pointwork at the Snaefell Summit terminus. Rather than the twin-bladed points generally used on railways the terminal stub is approached by single bladed point. The single blade pivots at the normal location of the crossing nose and swings across the full gauge of the line. This provides a sudden deviation in the line, rather than the smoothly curved deviation associated with standard pointwork. Naturally the cars are travelling at low speed when this point is used but there is a very noticeable sideways jolt as the bogies run onto, or off, the point blade. This point had been a feature of the line since it opened in 1895 and, when the track at the summit was re-laid in 2015, it was gratifying that the replacement track featured similar pointwork to the original. As the entire length (and weight) of the point rail has to be moved sideways when the point is changed, a geared capstan-style lever is provided: despite this, considerable physical effort is needed to switch the point. When Snaefell cars are stabled on the stub track at the summit the point is normally left in a central position, i.e., not aligned with either track, so that if the stabled car should move it will immediately derail between the two tracks rather than running away down the mountain (see page 47). All other pointwork on the Snaefell line is now composed of normal twin switch-bladed material.

Above: the unusual pointwork at the summit of the Snaefell line features this single-bladed configuration. The moveable rail has wheel flange contact from both sides and the channel below the rail slides on the lubricated steel plates on top of the sleepers (20 July 2017)

Left: the Fell rail is bent about its major axis at curves. A fishplated joint is bolted down to a support but the discontinuity in the curve is apparent. The sleeper on this side of the joint has no support, but the closest has its support held down by four bolts instead of the usual two (16 July 2017)

Above: the conductor leans hard on the capstan lever to overcome the friction forces of the single-blade point at the summit. The Summit Hotel, on the right, subsequently burnt down and was replaced by the current building. Sadly car 3 ran away from here in 2016 and was destroyed after de-railing near The Bungalow (Courtesy Travel Lens Photographic, 1960s)

Left: the original crossover installed on the uphill side at The Bungalow featured an interesting variation on the single-blade point configuration. On the left of the photograph is the long lever which swings the long single rail. Midway between the two tracks is a throw-over point lever, which rotates two short switch blades which are pivoted about two feet from the toe of the point. Both levers must be used to change the point. This variation gives a smoother ride through the point than that of the abrupt change in direction at the summit point (Courtesy Travel Lens Photographic, 1960s)

Right: the single-blade point by Dumbell's Row where the ascending and descending lines split featured another variation in the design. The lever on the left operates the short switch rails, which are similar to those at The Bungalow crossover, as well the long single blade. A single action to reset the point was required as every tram in normal service passed over this point needing frequent changes. The present day installation is a sprung point, so that the lever only needs to be pulled when a car is returning to the depot, wrong line from Laxey (Courtesy Travel Lens Photographic, June 1951)

Right: the approach to the Snaefell depot at Laxey seen from the rear of an ascending tram. The switch is set for the straight, but on the right can be seen the set of cranks which move the line segments to the curved position. In the background is the original two-road Snaefell car shed, and, on the left, the shed for the Wickham railcar belonging to NATS (Courtesy Travel Lens Photographic, June 1982)

Below: from a similar viewpoint to the photograph on the right, the line is now set for the depot approach track. The curve is not quite smooth and should be taken at slow speed. The overhead support here is unusual as a tubular cross bar spans between a pair of traction poles either side of the junction. (David Howard, Courtesy Travel Lens Photographic, c. 1950s)

When constructed, the use of single blade points on the SMR was standard practice, though very uncommon elsewhere. The crossover on the uphill side of The Bungalow was originally constructed with a matching pair of single-blade points, but these were replaced with standard turnouts when they became life expired, probably around 1980. In Laxey, the single line from the station splits into the ascending and descending lines immediately beyond the level crossing. The pointwork here was also single bladed but was also changed to a standard turnout, probably around the same time as The Bungalow crossover was replaced.

When the line was extended to the second Laxey station there was at least one point on the Snaefell line which maintained the continuity of the Fell rail through the point. This was where the depot approach road (formerly the approach to the first station) diverged from the new downhill track. In order to change the point a complex mechanism was provided which simultaneously moved both of the running rails plus the Fell rail bodily sideways in four sections, providing an approximation to a curve when aligned for the branch. Strictly speaking this was not a set of points in the accepted use of the words, but a slewable section of track which either aligned with the main line or the branch. Moving the mechanism was not a simple exercise due to the considerable weight of the rails that needed transferring. Although the pointwork from the downhill line to the depot was constructed in this way, it seems unlikely that there were other points of a similar design elsewhere, continuity of the Fell rail only being essential on a gradient. The preferred mode of operation was to dispatch all the cars likely to be needed on any one day from the depot and then change the point so that they could all descend to Laxey Station, rather than moving the rails more often than really necessary. This method of working continued into the twenty-first century, many years after the replacement and simplification of the complex trackwork meant that this was no longer operationally required. The pointwork was replaced in about 1983, after normal service braking had changed to rheostatic. All descending cars should stop at a board fixed immediately before the non-Fell rail fitted point (i.e., a point of normal design) leading to the depot, as the additional braking facility is absent for a short distance here.

The Snaefell line tends to suffer from rail creep. By the nature of the line, ascending cars are operating at high tractive effort and descending cars are using a high level of braking. In either case the wheel to rail friction forces attempt to push the rails downhill but the resilient nature of the rail fixings does not totally eliminate all movement. In consequence there is a tendency for the rail gaps to be reduced as a gradual downward migration of the rails occurs. On very hot days there can be an increased risk of track buckling due to high thermal compressive forces where the gaps have closed up. Remediation is simple in theory: the rails are released from their clips or spikes, pulled back up hill and resecured. Unfortunately this in not a practical solution as considerable work would be required to do this.

The Snaefell line presents many difficulties in maintenance. Road access to the line is only available at Laxey or The Bungalow so any material or personnel brought by road to these points must then carried up or down the line to the worksite. The trams can be used to propel wagons when required, but road-rail vehicles or wheeled tractors are also used when appropriate. Due to the seasonal nature of the line's operation, there is a preference for carrying out maintenance and renewals during the winter season, but even then the access requirements to the summit by NATS mean that at least one line of rails should be available at all times. Winter can also bring its own operational difficulties, after all 'Snaefell' is Norse for 'snow mountain'. This railway has many unique features and presents many interesting challenges in its continuing operation.

A more detailed view of the mechanism for changing the switch. The lever arms of the cranks vary along the length of the switch so that one pull on the handle moves each of the track segments laterally by different amounts. The result is an approximation to a curve by four straight line elements. The liberal coating of oil and grease on the steel plates on the top of the sleepers should make the pull easier (Courtesy Travel Lens Photographic, 1960s)

CHAPTER 3

EARTHWORKS

As with many tramways and light railways there are relatively few earthworks along the MER compared with the extensive cut-and-fill embankments and cuttings encountered on many heavy rail systems. On light railway systems the operational advantages of a less steeply graded and more direct route are often sacrificed for more economical construction. One of the major advantages of electric traction is its ability to operate on slopes as steep as 1 in 12 (8%) with no major difficulty. Gradients as steep as those of the MER would have been impractical to operate with steam power, and confirm that the line was always envisaged as a wholly electric system. One way of avoiding

Almost all the land seen here at the start of King Edward Road by Derby Castle terminus was reclaimed during the construction of the tramway and the adjoining road in 1892-3. Winter saloon 22 is running round trailer 42 prior to their next northbound departure (9 September 2006)

steep gradients is to follow the contours around hills and this feature is an inescapable part of the character and charm of the Manx Electric Railway. Sharp curves are more practicable on a narrow-gauge railway and the sinuous course pursued through the hills presents no major operational problems.

The major deviations from a more direct route between the termini are there to avoid large and expensive structures or earthworks. For example, the inland excursions to pass through Groudle Glen, Garwick Glen, Laxey and the Cornaa Valley all involve descents to cross valleys and re-ascents on the far side with near hairpin bends at the low points. At the northern end of the line a diversionary loop towards Maughold takes the line via Ballaskeig for a long and relatively steady drop down to the ultimate destination of Ramsey. The deviations to keep the gradients manageable on the Maughold loop are such that the 'northbound' line is actually running south east between Cornaa and Crowcreen.

To cross a valley there are two main possibilities. Most recognisable is the construction of a bridge or viaduct and there are several imposing examples along the line (see chapter 1). The alternative is the creation of an embankment which fills the gap with rock or soil. Bridges require detailed design by civil or structural engineers and can be impressive structures, but require construction components, materials and, in country areas, a skilled workforce to be brought to site. Temporary works can be major costs in their own right and require their own skill sets: for example, the wooden-framed centring for brick or stone arch bridges requires carpenters and joiners, while masons will cut and place the stonework. Bridges have a smaller footprint than embankments and this reduces the land take and hence purchase cost in already built up areas; against this their greater complexity in construction and potential long term maintenance costs has to be offset.

Embankments tend to be economic for relatively shallow crossings but the volume of rock or earth required increases as the square of the height, for example a 20ft high embankment needs sixteen times as much material as a 5ft high one. For a major construction, a ready source of suitable fill material is needed, otherwise haulage costs become excessive. Typically, masonry-lined culverts are installed at the foot of embankments so that any watercourses in the valley bottoms are not impeded and the water flow cannot erode and destabilize the embankments themselves. A typical embankment will be faced with earth, so that when it is covered with vegetation, it will eventually blend in with its background. Plant growth is encouraged on embankments as it enhances the embankment stability by reducing surface erosion from rainfall runoff as the plant roots form a cohesive mesh inside the earth. The generally rocky nature of the east coast of the Isle of Man provides an excellent source of fill, so that the MER embankments are inherently stable. This contrasts with the difficulties of construction and maintenance that can occur on lines through areas where the geology is dominated by clay or sedimentary deposits. Many of the Manx Electric Railway embankments are taken for granted because they are now well concealed by shrubs and bushes, but doubtlessly looked very raw when first constructed.

The view across the bay from Douglas Head shows the sheds at Derby Castle lying on the reclaimed land below the cliff face. The extent of the former inlet may be judged by the length of the concrete sea wall abutting the rocks (30 September 2017)

One of the most significant earthworks on the line is practically invisible nowadays. In order for the tramway to start at Derby Castle, adjacent to the existing terminus of the Douglas Horse Tramway, and work its way northwards, the inlet which lay at the northern end of Douglas Bay was filled in so that the new coast road and tramway could be constructed on the reclaimed ground. Inland of the line, the reclaimed area, formerly Port-y-Vada creek, became the site of Derby Castle depot which included the line's original power station, the car sheds and the engineering workshops that maintain the trams. Looking at this area across the bay from Douglas Head, the cliffs which lie behind the car sheds are now covered in vegetation with the illuminated 'Electric Railway' sign standing guard over the former inlet. Much of the fill material was obtained by blasting rock from the cliffs around Port Jack and below what is now King Edward Bay House, the site of which previously hosted the Douglas Bay Hotel.

To provide a suitable foundation for the track bed and the road to Howstrake it was necessary to cut back the cliff, and these works are

Near the summit of the line at Howstrake the road and tramway are cut into the cliffs below the King Edward Bay Golf course; the golf course is not apparent at the top of the cliffs (4 May 2004)

evident from the rock face on the inland side of the tramway. The road and the tramway were constructed concurrently as part of the scheme to develop the Howstrake Estate, but to the untrained eye the coastal road approach to Douglas from the north may seem much older than it is. The new coast road was originally called The Marine Drive, not to be confused with the road of the same name between Douglas Head and Port Soderick. Following the visit of His Royal Highness and Queen Alexandra in 1902, and their journey on the MER to Ramsey, it was renamed King Edward Road. Over the years considerable housing development has taken place inland of the tramway and much of the area between Onchan Village and King Edward Road is now effectively a suburb.

Beyond Groudle Glen the promoters, now constituted as The Douglas and Laxey Coast Electric Tramway Company, built the tramline and the parallel road to Halfway simultaneously, continuing the route which they had previously built from Derby Castle. As the line was constructed through largely open countryside, whose owners were sympathetic to the development, the selected route provides a steady climb with no major earthworks.

North of Baldrine is Garwick Glen and the tramway deviates inland away from the main road, and crosses a major earthwork structure which straddles the head of the glen. The scale of the works is most evident by looking down into the now privately-owned glen about 60ft (20m) below the tramway. The undergrowth now largely obscures the glen inland of the tramway. Fill material for the embankment was probably sourced from cutting the tramway into the hillside on the north of the glen. The stream which flows through the glen, and previously powered the mill, is carried beneath the embankment in a masonry culvert.

On the way to Laxey the line generally follows the edge of the hills above Laxey Bay and there are no major earthworks of note, although some cutting into the steep hillside was necessary between Ballabeg and South Cape. The line is cut into the south side of the Laxey Valley as it descends into Glen Roy.

North of Laxey Station the earthworks become more prevalent. There is a major stone-faced embankment, which also carries the New Road, over the Laxey River, shortly after the line leaves the station. The embankment adjoins the old washing floors of the Great Laxey Mine and it is probable that the embankment was constructed from mine waste which was to hand from the spoil heaps. On the north side of the valley the now restored Great Laxey Mines steam railway passes below the MER in the Isle of Man's sole railway 'tunnel', although in reality this is a stone-lined arched way left through the embankment. In engineering terms a tunnel is excavated through rock or earth without breaking the surface, although, as here, the term is sometimes used to describe structures which have been buried subsequently. The Laxey River is accommodated in a separate, and much larger, masonry-lined culvert on the south side of the valley, the opposite side from the Mines Railway. The embankment here contrasts with the masonry viaduct that carries the tramway across Glen Roy between Laxey car sheds and Laxey Station (see pages 17-8); a very different solution a short distance away.

North of Laxey the track runs below but almost parallel to the Ramsey Road, having performed a complete U turn from the approach to Laxey on the south side of the river. The line is cut into the valley side with an embankment section where Minorca Hill is crossed by a viaduct, the line looming above the adjacent properties. Small sections of

The massive embankment which carries the MER and the New Road over the Laxey Valley looms over the former washing floors of the Great Laxey Mine. The MER is about 90ft (27.5m) above the river, which is out of view on the left of the photograph. The wooden hut on the terrace is the station of the restored Great Laxey Mines Railway. When working, the ore was brought here, through the tunnel under the embankment, and tipped down to the washing floors. The MER traction poles are visible on the skyline (7 February 2019)

Left: both the main road and the tramway run on a ledge blasted from the cliff at Bulgham. The retaining wall and parapet separate the highway and the cliff on the right is covered in stainless steel netting to prevent rock falls. The sea is about 500ft (150m) below the tram (20 July 2014)

Below: the retaining wall which collapsed in 1967 seen from the footpath leading from Dhoon Glen stop to the beach. The bus and tram stop flags at Ballaragh are fixed to the short pole seen on the left of the picture, locating this wall about a quarter of a mile from the summit curve. The maximum height of the embankment is about 70ft (20m) (9 August 2018)

cutting follow around the Laxey North Headland after which the line climbs steadily towards the summit of the line at Bulgham.

The final part of the ascent to the highest point of the line at Bulgham is constructed on a ledge cut into the cliffs. On the inland side, the main coast road, which predates the MER, once again runs parallel to the tramway. In places the cliffs needed to be cut back further, and the road moved inland to give space for the tramway's extension. At Bulgham, rock falls from the cliffs have long been a hazard to both road and tramway. In the early twenty-first century work to reduce the rock fall danger has included the provision of wire netting, held in place by rock

Slightly below the summit at Bulgham but looking down from the clifftop, the terraces cut into the rock face for the tramway and the coast road are clearly visible. Retaining walls help support the rights of way, though buttresses are not needed (7 May 2004)

bolts and stainless steel cables, these contain minor falls and reduce the potential for boulders to fall onto the road, the tramway or their users. Rock bolting involves drilling sufficiently far into the rock to find stable substrate. A steel rod is inserted into the hole and grouted in place, after which the rod is tensioned by tightening a nut on the screw-threaded outer end of the rod. This restrains the less stable rock on the outer face.

Part of the lower end of the line leading up to Bulgham is supported on substantial masonry abutments. At this point there is a cleft in the cliff face: a masonry supporting structure was a more economic solution than removing a substantial length of cliff face to bring the road and tramway further inland. The outer parapet of this section carries a decorative railing.

Following the partial collapse of this retaining wall, on 20 January 1967, the through service on the MER was immediately suspended. Two temporary stations, with crossovers, were hastily opened on either side of the breach and an extra five minutes added to the through journey time. This allowed passengers to transfer between the two stations by a short walk along the road, which was still available for foot traffic. Road traffic was diverted between Laxey and Dhoon Glen via the old road through Ballaragh.

If no remedial works had been undertaken the tramway would have closed, but there would have been no guarantee that the adjacent main road was stable and loss of both the road and tramway would have been grossly inconvenient. In a collaborative effort between the Highways Board and the MER, a major project to stabilize the supporting structure with a complex arrangement of piles was followed through. Specialist piling contractors installed a total of 116 diagonally-inclined 3" diameter concrete piles below the tramway in four parallel double rows and grouted into place. The effect was to build an intersecting network of strengthening piles into the substrate. The work was planned and executed with commendable speed, as the line reopened throughout on 10 July 1967 and through services were restored immediately. Continued monitoring of the retaining wall supporting the tramway is required to ensure its long term stability and the safe operation of this part of the line.

The cutting at Ballagorry seen looking south from the bridge. When the line opened in 1898 there was only a single track through the cutting, an expedient move to open the line, but operationally inconvenient. Presumably further excavation was needed to accommodate the second track which enabled the bottleneck to be removed (13 September 2015)

The next major earthworks are at Dhoon Glen, just to the north of the station and refreshment hut, where the tramway and the coast road again share an embankment which crosses the stream that flows down to Dhoon beach. This earth structure stands about 35ft (10m) high and is built on a gentle curve. The material for building the embankment was probably obtained from the works which cut the tramway into the hill on the south side of Dhoon Glen. Shortly inland of the embankment the glen splits into two branches, with a substantial middle ground between them. Taking the line further inland here would have reduced the amount of fill required, but this would have been offset by the requirement to cut the further into the hills either side the glen. Optimal design aims to balance the cut and fill requirements to minimize excavation and local transport costs.

Along the next stretch of line there are many relatively minor stream crossings passing under the MER, near Burns Crossing, Dhoon Farm, Dhoon Quarry, Ballig and Glen Mona each of which has a masonry culvert beneath their embankments. Due to the verdant vegetation along the line these features are not all immediately obvious to the casual passenger but may be seen from the adjacent road. These would have been constructed to a standard design and the contractors would have worked along the line.

When designing embankments or cuttings, slope stability is the main requirement. A cutting through rock can have steep sides as the material can be self supporting, such as the cliff face at Bulgham. Rock is also a good material for embankment formation as individual blocks lock against each other and a slope of around 45 degrees is practical. Stable slopes with sandy soil, which are largely formed of granular material, are difficult to maintain as a slope of around 20 degrees to the horizontal is required, meaning that cuttings and embankments need to be relatively wide. Although easy to dig, relatively large volumes need to excavated or placed. Cohesive soils, which have an extremely fine grain structure, such as clays can also be problematic as they are very sensitive to the presence of pore water: sudden failure by slipping is possible after prolonged periods of rain. Many soils lie between the two extreme of sand (granular) and clay (cohesive) and testing to determine their characteristics is needed before deciding on a suitable design slope. Fortunately, much of the underlying geology of the MER is rock which is inherently stable. Problem areas tend to be those close to the coast where wave action can encourage cliff falls.

Shortly after leaving The Garey the line climbs to Ballagorry and then drops into a relatively long and deep cutting to pass under the tramway's only overbridge (see page 19). The cutting, between Ballagorry and Watson's Crossing (see photograph on page 57) is the most significant one on the line. The cutting's sides are steep, showing that it has been excavated from stable rock. The cutting sees little sunshine and following rain the rails can remain wet: the steep slope occasionally causing trams to suffer wheel spin. Liberal use of the sanding gear is sometimes necessary. The line emerges from the cutting at Watson's Crossing in the Cornaa Valley. The Ballagorry bridge marks the point at which the tramway and the coast road to Ramsey diverge from each other: the road takes a shorter but much hillier course, while the tramway traverses a relatively sparsely populated farming area to reach the same destination.

An embankment supports the line as it passes the former Ballaglass power station, which lies on the inland side. Major winter storms and heavy rainfall have caused problems with the stability of this embankment and in recent years remedial works have been carried out. Additional drainage was added on the coastal side of the line, with discharge through pipework below the line. Meanwhile the embankment was cleared of all undergrowth so that strengthening could carried out below the line.

Immediately after Ballaglass halt a further substantial embankment structure carries the tracks over the stream which previously supplied water to the nearby power station, and which flows through Ballaglass Glen and out to

Above: at the head of Ballaglass Glen the tramway is carried over the Cornaa River on this embankment with a stone culvert supporting the line. This is a major stone arch with a diameter of about 20ft (6m) and a length of about 50ft (15m). The embankment places a surcharge on the arch, putting the masonry rings into compression. In the operating season the foliage will largely conceal the structure (9 April 2017)

Below: looking at the embankment in the photograph on the left, from the shelter for Ballaglass Glen, winter saloon 19 leads trailer 47 on their way south. The stone-arched culvert lies below the short straight section of track at the middle of the S bend and is immediately in front of the tram. The structure is indeed inconspicuous (9 April 2017)

sea at Port Cornaa. The sharp S bend here switches the line from one side of the glen to the other. Although the line runs on an impressive embankment structure the passenger needs to disembark from the tram and walk down into Ballaglass Glen to see the full scale of the works and the masonry arch which bridges the stream. Viewed from a passing tram the close packed trees conceal the size of the drop to the valley floor.

There are only minor earthworks on the section between Ballaglass and Lewaigue as the tramway generally follows the contours as it loops around the hills. Minor cuttings or small earthworks where the line is cut into the side of the hill are all that are seen. The drop down to Ramsey continues with minor earthworks in the vicinity of Bellevue.

Above: at Ballagorry Manx Rail Projects' diesel locomotive Pig *is seen on the seaside line with materials for the enhanced drainage works being installed half a mile away near the former Ballaglass power station (13 September 2015)*

Between Bellevue and Ballure the line runs close to the clifftop and this is an area which required extensive cliff stabilization works during 2012-4. There was only a narrow strip of land between the coast road and the cliffs so this was the only practical route here. Wave erosion of the cliffs had threatened the stability of the line, and extensive piling was carried out here to reinforce the cliff face. The lower part of the cliff face has also been protected with a substantial bank of rock armour on the seashore side. The job was finished with rock dumping on the beach itself so that wave action on the protective bank is eliminated. The cliff height here is around 100ft (35m). With working on the beach to deliver and install the rock armour

Right: looking along the beach at Ballure from Ramsey Pier, protective material is being added to the cliffs at Ballure. The finished height of the mound on which the cherry picker is located will be about 50% more than seen here. Tipping material from the top was not an option, so it was brought along the beach. The tramway passes close to the cliff edge (27 September 2013)

Left: the Ballure works in their completed state. A winter saloon heads downhill towards Ramsey above the substantial deposit of gravel and the rock armour at beach level. The rock armour's random appearance will dissipate the energy of breaking waves and minimize erosion of the ballast it is guarding (15 August 2017)

only being possible with favourable tides and weather conditions, the placement of an estimated 12,000 tonnes of ballast for the bank, and around the same for the large rocks at the base was a serious exercise in logistics. In addition, the many bored piles used to stabilize the cliff make this a major project, probably approaching the £1,000,000 mark. Although the trams pass within a few feet there is nothing to see from a seat on board.

When the MER extension to Ramsey was first mooted the engineers planned to take the line from Dreemskerry down to the coast at Port-e-Vullen and run below the cliffs at Ballure to join the Queen's Promenade in Ramsey near Queen's Pier. This final mile would have given the MER a seawall approach to Ramsey. It is thought that, when the engineers surveyed the route, the cliff instabilities caused them to change their plans and the current route was selected. The line would have needed a long section across the valley bottom between Dreemskerry and Port-e-Vullen: this area is often waterlogged or flooded following winter storms and this section would have needed a considerable amount of ground reinforcement to build a stable track bed. In Victorian days this could have taken the form of placing layers of brushwood until a sufficiently stable surface was established for the permanent way. The difficulty is that the amount of brushwood needed could not have been known in advance. In the twenty-first century blocks of expanded polystyrene foam have been used to form strong, but light, embankments capable of carrying trunk roads. By spreading the vehicle loads sufficiently widely the weak soil is not overloaded. Forming a trackbase to Port-e-Vullen would have been a stark contrast to the predictability of the foundations of the majority of the MER, which is rarely far from the underlying rock of the eastern side of the island.

On the seafront at Port Lewaigue is the start of the sea-wall section of the originally proposed MER route to Ramsey. Somewhat improbably the houses are 'The Moorings'. These were constructed by the tramway as guest houses but sold on as private residences after the financial reconstruction in 1902 (27 January 2019)

Shortly after the now-stabilized clifftop the line crosses the major structure of the Ballure Viaduct (see pages 20-1), and the final light-controlled crossing of the A2 coast road. Immediately beyond the level crossing, there is a retaining wall on the inland side which supports a minor road that leads to the Ramsey Hairpin on the Mountain Road. The final earthworks are between Queen's Drive West and the line's ultimate destination of Ramsey. The trackbed is cut into the hill on the left, with the spoil forming an embankment, as it runs above the back gardens of the houses in Waterloo Road.

With a few exceptions the earthworks along the line rarely draw attention to themselves. The main exceptions are the spectacular cliff edge ride at Bulgham, the embankments across the Laxey valley and Dhoon Glen. If there are no problems, then the grassy banks with their mature vegetation have blended with their background. It is only when problems emerge, for instance due to water-driven erosion following heavy winter storms, that attention focuses on them. At times of exceptionally heavy rainfall there are a few locations where the line may flood, such Lewaigue and Cornaa, and the service may be temporarily suspended: getting muddy water in tramcar motors is not recommended. Maintenance of the lineside ditches and drains may not generate as much enthusiast interest as restoring a vintage tramcar but such work is an integral part of tramway operation.

SNAEFELL MOUNTAIN RAILWAY

The first earthwork of note on the SMR is the vicarage wall. When the line was extended from the Dumbell's Row terminus to the new joint station with the MER, part of the vicarage garden was taken by the railways and a masonry retaining wall built to support the remainder. This wall is adjacent to the level crossing outside Laxey station. The miners' houses of Dumbell's Row had already been built when the SMR was constructed so this section was cut into the hillside behind them.

The earthworks on the Snaefell Mountain Railway consist principally of ledges cut into the side of the Laxey Valley (for the line below The Bungalow) or the side of the mountain itself (for the line above The Bungalow); the ledges will be treated generically as they are a dominating feature of the line. At Bungalow the line levels out as it crosses the saddle point formed by the heads of the Laxey and Sulby Valleys. Here the Mountain Road, part of the TT race course, is crossed by a level crossing. The surveyed line of the route was designed to follow the Laxey Valley and then spiral round the mountain ascending at a near constant rate of climb between Laxey and the summit. The ruling gradient is 1 in 12 (8.5%) which means that the line can be

Above: the vicarage wall at Laxey looms over Snaefell car 4 as it heads towards the summit. The wall is about 20ft (6m) high and carries similar castellations to the nearby bridges and viaducts on the MER. Land was taken for the MER extension to Ramsey as well as to provide access to Laxey station for the SMR. (4 May 2008)

Above: the bulk of the retaining walls, with their buttresses, at Lhergy Veg seen from across the Laxey Valley. On the left is the only flat section of line between Laxey and The Bungalow. The transition to the ruling gradient on the right is noticeable and is not *due to lens distortion (9 June 2017)*

Left: looking from the cab of an ascending tram at Lhergy Veg, with the level piece of track in front of the tram. The recommencement of the climb is abrupt. The retaining wall and the buttresses can be seen on the Laxey Valley side of the line. Blasting the shoulder of the hill to the left would have been a major piece of work, and it is likely that on balance supporting the track with the retaining wall was a more economic proposition (20 July 2017)

Downhill of the mountain road crossing at The Bungalow the remedial works carried out after the December 2015 storm damage are taking shape. Single-line working is in effect on the left of the orange fencing which denotes the edge of the work site. The tops of the H-section steel piles are on the right. The wooden T pieces are left by the setting-out surveyors and used to set the rail heights and offsets. Fell rail from the damaged track is still on site and may be re-installed or replaced in due course (23 April 2016)

worked by adhesion, without the need to resort to more complex means of traction. As the line is cut into the mountain it is almost entirely supported on the underlying rock which is a permanent way engineer's dream: a good solid base with a high degree of implicit stability.

In order to reduce the construction costs there are, of course, departures from the steady rate of climb. At Lhergy Veg, about halfway between Laxey and The Bungalow, there is a short section of level track where the line is supported by a major retaining wall on the valley side. It is sometimes stated that this short section is inclined in the opposite direction to the prevailing gradient, but this is an optical illusion. The retaining wall is about 25ft (8m) high and the buttresses are about 7ft (2m) square and built from local stone. In the lower sections the line crosses a number of minor streams which drain from the surrounding farmland towards the Laxey River. Special action, with concrete-lined channels and culverts under the line, has been taken to ensure that the drained water is carried away safely without eroding the embankment sections here.

Looking from the valley side, the form and scale of the reinstatement works incorporating H-section steel piles with concrete infill panels, is clearly visible. Following pile installation the tops have been flame cut and await recovery. Ballast has been placed and the track relaid (23 April 2016)

Severe winter storms, such as those of early December 2015, can cause a significant amount of slippage and washouts in the embankments over the length of line. Single-line working was required between Laxey and Bungalow during the first half of the 2016 season while essential repair works were carried out. At Lhergy Veg a temporary connexion was installed where the ascending (valley side) track was swung over to join the other track while major works were carried out on the ascending line above and the descending line below this point. Without this measure it would not have been possible to operate during the first half of the season. The major work in early 2016 involved strengthening and reconstructing a considerable length of the embankments on the lower half of the line. H-section steel piles were driven on the valley side of the line where washouts had occurred. New ballast fill material, supported by concrete panels between the piles, was added between this area and the inner track. The piles were driven until they reached the required resistance and the excess steel was flame cut to leave the tops at the required level to support the panels. Finally new outer track was laid on top of the newly filled area and the line was able to be re-opened on both tracks. In addition, improved drainage, with much higher flow capacity concrete culverts, was added below Lhergy Veg.

The earthworks along the SMR show little variation. Being built through open country the builders had freedom to adopt a consistent and economical approach which would have minor impact on the local populace. The work on the line started in January 1895, with the line opening on 21 August of the same year. Taking well under a year to construct a unique railway was a considerable achievement.

Downhill from the former power station the work is not quite so far advanced. On the right a barrage of gabions (ballast filled steel cages) is supporting the embankment. The setting-out guides show the elevation relative to the ordnance datum of the top of the T and also the chainage. Although measured in metres, the old terminology is still in use. Note: to take the pictures on this page, the photographer was on site with permission and Personal Protective Equipment (PPE) (23 April 2016)

CHAPTER 4

POWER SUPPLY

In the early years, the provision of electric power to the Manx Electric and Snaefell Mountain Railways was driven by the rapidly evolving technologies and the economies that could be made by adopting them. Initially, direct current (DC) power at line voltage was produced locally at several sites, supplemented by accompanying banks of wet cell batteries to provide load balancing. Within a decade of the opening in 1893, the DC technology was obsolete and, by 1904, replacement by high-tension alternating current (AC) plant with local rotary convertor (transformer-rectifier) units had largely superseded the earlier installations. By the 1930s the Manx Electricity Board grid had made electricity widely available on the island. In late 1934 the MER agreed to take all its supplies from the grid, finally ceasing to generate its own power by May 1935. As part of the changeover, the rotary convertors were supplanted by more modern and economical mercury-arc rectifiers. After the major changes of the first four decades of the tramway, the electrical supply evolution has not been quite so rapid or dramatic: the final mercury-arc rectifier was only switched out at Groudle in late 2017, after more than eighty years of service. Solid-state equipment has now swept all else away. Unless there is a breakthrough in technology, such systems seem set for a long reign.

When the first part of the line which became the Manx Electric Railway was promoted, the provision of electric power to the public in the British Isles was almost non-existent. Indeed, the Isle of Man Tramways and Electric Power Company was one of the earliest suppliers of electricity on the island, albeit only within a restricted area near the new plant at Derby Castle. This was a simple case of necessity being the mother of invention. A coastal route, operated by steam power, running north from Douglas would either have needed an uneconomic amount of cuttings, embankments and bridges or would have been too steeply graded. Therefore, electric power was the only practical solution. The use of such cutting-edge technology in 1893, when only a handful of electric tramways and railways were operating in Great Britain, was a massive leap of faith by the line's promoters. If electricity was needed, and there were no existing supplies, it would have to be produced in house for local use. Having the means of producing electricity led to marketing the product to third parties within range of the power station, and a supplementary source of revenue.

The former power station building off Glen Road in Laxey (see page 64). This was the boiler house; the chimney stood to the right of this building on the upstream side of the plant. The river flows under the bridge from which the photograph is taken, but the feedwater, drawn from the weir upstream to the right, passed behind the building (12 November 2017)

In those early days electricity was generated using direct current (DC) dynamos at the required line voltage. Low voltage DC is impractical to transmit over long distances as the energy losses, due to the electrical resistance of the cabling, mean that the voltage drop more than a few miles away from the generating station would be so large as to make the concept unserviceable. The power transmitted is the product of the voltage and the current, but the electrical losses are proportional to the current squared. For a given level of power transmission the ideal solution is to transmit at the highest practical voltage with a correspondingly low current. For example, if the voltage is increased by a factor of ten then the power loss reduces to one per cent of the original.

The first power station was situated on the newly reclaimed land at Derby Castle, supplied by imported coal brought by cart from Douglas harbour. Water supplies were drawn from the streams that had flowed into Port-y-Vada. The combined watercourse still emerges into Douglas Bay, but through a pipe in the sea wall. Water fed two Galloway boilers, so named after the brothers who formed the company, 20ft (6.1m) long and 6ft (1.83m) diameter operating at 120psi. These in turn powered two 90hp Galloway vertical compound engines with 10in (254mm) (high pressure) and 18in (457mm) (low pressure) diameter cylinders of 20in (508mm) stroke. Running at 150rpm these drove Mather and Platt Manchester dynamos, a trade name referring to the company's hometown, producing 100 Amperes at 500 Volts (DC), i.e. 50kW per unit. The station switchgear was also supplied by Mather and Platt, who were the electrical engineering contractors for the line. In the following year, to meet the increased power demand for the extension to Laxey, this plant was augmented with a third Galloway boiler and an extra generator, which was of a more advanced design, again supplied by Mather and Platt. This had the field coils above the armature instead of at the sides and it proved to be more efficient.

Derby Castle supplied electricity for the initial section of line, opened in 1893, to Groudle Glen, which was a little over two miles away and hence sufficiently close that there were no DC voltage drop problems. A wet cell battery house was constructed at Groudle Glen. Although the Derby Castle installation was capable of supplying the average power requirements of the short line, it was unable to support two cars simultaneously starting uphill: the stored energy in the batteries catered for this eventuality. As the line was originally single track with a mid-point passing loop meeting the peak demand was a high priority. Electric power was also made available for non-railway uses in the Onchan area and was a profitable business in its own right - hence justifying the 'Electric Power' in the company title, 'Isle of Man Tramways and Electric Power Company'.

The power plant at Derby Castle had a short life, being removed in 1903 when the new high-tension AC generation and distribution system superseded the original equipment. Derby Castle became home to a substation supplied by the new 7000V AC feeder system from the Laxey power station. The new substations commissioned as part of the scheme contained rotary converters, supplied by Kolben and Co of Prague, which ran at 500rpm and were rated at 150kW at 330/550V. They were designed for alternative compound or simple wound operation and fed by pairs of 75kW Kolben transformers. A stone substation was built at Groudle Glen and two rotary converters were installed there adjacent to the existing battery house.

The 1894 extension from Groudle Glen to Laxey required a new source of power, and to meet this, a second power station was constructed just off Glen Road in Laxey, using the Laxey River as a source of boiler and cooling water. The new plant was equipped with two sets of Galloway boilers, compound steam engines, and Mather and Platt dynamos identical to the additional set installed at Douglas at the same time. The new Laxey plant fed the northern section of line, while that at Derby Castle continued to supply the southern end.

The Laxey and Snaefell mines were in operation at this time and there was a substantial export trade in lead and zinc ores through Laxey harbour. The import of coal stocks, brought by steamer for the tramway, increased activity in the then industrialized valley. The new power station was about half a mile upstream of the harbour but on the opposite side of the river from Glen Road, which was used to bring cartloads of coal from the harbour.

In order to balance the electrical load, a substantial wet cell battery installation was constructed adjoining the new generating plant. The batteries were charged during periods of low traction demand and discharged during periods of high traffic, thereby reducing the peak generating requirement. This meant that the power station operated at a steadier and more economical rate, but that the overhead line voltage could be maintained throughout the day. Above the power station, adjoining the northbound tram track, a water tower was constructed in 1916-7: distilled water from the power station condensers could be collected from the water tower for distribution to the other battery installations along the line and used for topping up the cells. This tank still stands, incongruously resembling the remains of a water tower for steam locomotives, which of course it never was.

During the summer the trees beside the line conceal the power station building which lies in the valley below, only about 100 yards (90m) away. Some visitors wonder what purpose this structure served. It is the water tower where distilled water, pumped up the slope, was offloaded, into containers carried on goods trucks, for distribution to the load balancing battery installations at Ballaglass and Groudle (7 January 2018)

Extensions to the scope of operations of the tramway system saw the construction of the Snaefell Mountain Railway over the winter of 1894-5. Once again the additional route mileage required the installation of extra generating capacity, this time in the form of a plant about half way up the mountain line. The voltage drop on the final section to the summit would have been excessive for a DC supply drawn solely from Laxey at the foot of the line. All materials for the Snaefell power station's construction were carried on the mountain road to Bungalow and lowered to the site - obviously there was no access from Laxey as the tramway had not yet been built.

The remains of the disused Snaefell power station around the mid-point of the mountain line. The uphill end of the generator building survives, having been used as a substation. The redundant boiler has been left in situ *when the boiler house was demolished. The coal slide was roughly where the photographer is standing and the coal shed was on the downhill side of the boiler house (23 April 2016)*

The Snaefell power station was equipped with four Galloway Boilers of 26ft (7.9m) long and 6ft (1.8m) diameter and five Mather and Platt compound horizontal engines with 16in (406mm) (HP) and 20in (508mm) (LP) cylinders of 16in (406mm) stroke. Each of these was coupled to a 60kW Hopkinson-designed Mather and Platt dynamo. Being near the top of a mountain there was no ready water supply so this was fed through a 2in (51mm) main from a small steam-powered pumping station on the Sulby River below Tholt-y-Will a couple of miles or so away on the far side of the hill. Presumably pumping water from the much closer Laxey Valley was impracticable as supplying a low-level pumping station with fuel would not have been easy; possibly the rights to the Laxey Valley water may have belonged to the nearby Snaefell Mine. An additional battery house was installed adjacent to the Snaefell car shed above Laxey with a 560 Ampere-hour rating. This could be interconnected with the similar installation about half a mile away in Laxey power station, enabling occasional works trams to run out of season without the need to fire the boilers on the mountain section.

The rusting remains of one of the Galloway boilers from the Snaefell plant are still visible from the Mountain Railway shortly below the crossing of the Mountain Road at The Bungalow. The flues from the power station passed below the tracks, exhausting through a chimney on the far side of the line. The chimney base is still visible, but the

The replica of SMR car 7, Maria, is in Laxey Station. Behind is a low loader labelled 'S.P. Carter Heavy Haulage Baldrine'. Presumably the replica has just been offloaded. (Courtesy Travel Lens Photographic, August 1995)

chimney has been demolished. Following a period of use as an electrical substation some of the power station buildings remain.

Sufficient coal for the operating season was stockpiled at the mountain plant before the start of the summer tourist service. Fuel supplies were ferried up from Laxey by freight tram 7, also known as *Maria*, which had a large wagon-like load area between its two end cabs. *Maria's* power bogies were borrowed from a passenger car, usually number 5, for the winter, and returned before the tourist season began.

As part of the high-tension AC scheme, one of the Mather and Platt sets was removed in 1904 and a rotary convertor installed in its place, with power being supplied from Laxey. The remaining generating plant was retained for seasonal use, only being decommissioned near the end of the 1924 season when a second rotary convertor was installed, again supplied with 7000V AC directly from the Laxey plant.

The completion of the MER line to Ramsey in 1898-9 increased the tramways' electricity supply requirements yet again, and a further power station was constructed at Ballaglass, approximately mid-way between Laxey and Ramsey. The stream which flows down the Cornaa valley, before finding its way through Ballaglass Glen to the sea at Port Cornaa, supplied water for the boilers and cooling system. Two more Galloway boilers were installed, supplying steam to a pair of Robb Armstrong tandem compound engines at 120psi giving an indicated horse power of 180 each. At 175 rpm the Electrical Construction Company (ECC) six-pole generators produced 240 Amperes at 500V (i.e. 120kW) from their 51in (1295mm) by 16.5in (420mm) armatures.

The rebuilt Snaefell goods tram, number 7, Maria, *and a wagon with tank load stand in Laxey station during the Isle of Man Railways celebrations for the 125th year of the opening of the steam railway. This tram formed the basis of the MER diesel-electric locomotive number 34 (4 May 1998)*

A booster set giving 500V/150V was also supplied and was used for charging the cells in the new battery house adjacent to the power plant, which provided load-balancing capabilities similar to those already present at Laxey and Groudle Glen. The battery could supply 140 Amperes for six hours.

The tramway proposed to install a hydro-electric plant at Ballaglass with a weir near the MER bridge, adjacent to the stop at the top of the glen, with the turbine located 1470ft (450m) downstream. Such a plant would have enabled the batteries at Ballaglass to be charged and would have reduced the demand on the boilers, especially during the off-peak season. At the time Ballaglass was an unspoiled wooded glen: the hydro-electric scheme was not followed through, and Ballaglass Glen's natural beauty remains to this day.

At this time the MER purchased three Bonner wagons, each comprising a four-wheeled cart which could be loaded onto or removed from matching wagon underframes by a ramp. This avoided the need for costly transhipment of loads between road and rail. 'Piggy-backing' road vehicles by rail is still used by the Channel Tunnel. Coal for Ballaglass was landed at the quayside in Ramsey. From there it was conveyed, by road, in the Bonner wagons, which were then loaded onto their railway underframes for travel by the MER to Ballaglass. Initially, loading was at Ramsey Station but this was changed to Queen's Drive following complaints about noise from local residents. Coal was discharged down the embankment at Ballaglass directly into the plant's bunkers. Other uses for the Bonner wagons could have been granite setts from the quarries at Dhoon or Ballajora for export from either Douglas or Ramsey harbours, but the wagons could have been used more widely. Unfortunately two of the Bonner wagons and the MER electric locomotive, number 23 (see pages 85 and 90), were destroyed in an accident on 24 January 1914. The train ran away while descending towards Laxey from the north and overturned on a bend above Minorca which is still known as 'Bonner Corner'. The fate of the third Bonner Wagon is not known. Following the loss of the Bonner wagons transhipment of coal between road and rail would have been necessary to continue to discharge down the embankment at Ballaglass. Ballaglass was equipped with a rotary converter in the 1904 high-tension scheme and 7000V AC current was supplied from Laxey via overhead cables. Although the generators were still in place, Ballaglass only needed to use these during peak periods.

Right: *in the Laxey Valley the supports for the pipe which led water to the hydro-electric plant are still in place adjacent to the river, on its south side. These are about half way between the steam power plant and The Shore Hotel (12 November 2017)*

Below: *more than eighty years since the hydro-electric generators were decommissioned the building that housed them is still in good condition. This is a short distance upstream from The Shore Hotel on the south bank of the Laxey River. The sack hoist above the end doorway is formed of an inverted length of rail (12 November 2017)*

The generating capacity at Laxey was also increased when the Ramsey extension was constructed in 1898: the Ballaglass plant was designed to supply the northern part of the extension, with the southern part being supplied from Laxey. Additional steam-powered plant was installed at Laxey, comprising an additional Galloway boiler and a Robb Armstrong compound engine with directly-coupled generator similar to the new pair located at Ballaglass. At the same time, but nearly a quarter of a mile downstream from the Laxey steam plant, a hydro-electric generating plant was built, incorporating two 70hp Victor water turbines on a single shaft running at 720rpm, and driving a bipolar dynamo generating 160 Amperes at 520V. This was electrically connected to the steam plant upstream and controlled remotely by a pair of Lundell quarter horsepower motors. This was an early instance of renewable energy being used by a transport company and one which would be considered very green nowadays. The modest hydro-electric plant was installed in a masonry building a few hundred yards upstream of The Shore Hotel.

Water was supplied to the hydro-electric plant by diverting it into a channel from above a weir situated on the Laxey River a short distance downstream of the Laxey Woollen Mills near the top of Glen Road. The water channel passed behind the steam power station and then entered a 3ft (915mm) diameter pipeline which ran close to the southern river bank. A couple of settling tanks *en route* removed extraneous sediment from the water. This scheme gave a 26ft (7.9m) head at the turbine centreline and the draft tube added a further 15ft (4.6m) of effective head. The tailrace led back to the Laxey River with discharge above the bridge in Old Laxey. At the time of writing the channel behind the building of the steam plant still carries water and, although the pipe has been removed, a series of masonry pipe supports remains in place adjacent to the riverside path.

The decision by the MER to change to high-tension three-phase AC distribution brought further changes to the Laxey plant which was selected as the hub of the new system, becoming operational in July 1903. In the main steam plant two new Climax

Running behind the old steam power station in Laxey is this leat which led from the weir and fed into the pipework leading to the hydro-electric plant (12 November 2017)

cylindrical vertical boilers were installed, 12ft (3.6m) diameter by 23ft (7m) high operating at 165psi. Weir feed pumps and Mirlees and Watson condensing equipment were used. These fed two Bellis Morcom triple expansion 400hp engines with 13in (330mm) stroke and cylinders of 12, 17 and 26in (305, 432 and 660mm) diameter. Star-connected 300kW revolving field alternators supplied by Société Électricité et Hydraulique de Charleroi in Belgium completed the upgrade. (In a star connexion with a balanced load in each phase, no independent return wires are needed: all three wires are connected together as the net return current is always zero.) The Galloway boiler with the Robb Armstrong engine was retained, but the surplus 1894 Mather and Platt equipment was offered for sale.

From Laxey, 7000V was taken through new feeders to new substations at Douglas, Groudle, Ballaglass and Snaefell, as well as one inside Laxey power station itself. Kolben of Prague supplied pairs of 75kW transformers feeding rotary convertors rated at 150kW for each site (see page 64).

Traffic on the MER was, of course, far higher in the tourist season, and the hope was that the water turbine at Laxey, operating in conjunction with the batteries, would provide adequate power during the winter season to allow the steam plant to be shut down. The plan was that the Laxey steam plant would run from 6:30am to midnight in summer only. In practice, intermittent usage was required about every three weeks in winter to make up any deficiency of the hydro-electric plant in keeping the batteries charged.

In 1914 the MER acquired a second-hand 750kW (1000hp) turbo-alternator which it planned to use at Laxey. Due to the outbreak of war, and the consequent loss of tourist traffic, this plan was shelved for the duration and the turbo-alternator was stored in Laxey goods shed. Dating from 1906 this was a relatively new piece of equipment which was finally installed, on a gantry, at Laxey in 1920. As it produced 400V at 25 cycles, a step-up transformer, built by the British Electric Transformer Co. of Hayes, provided the required 7000V to be compatible with the existing system. A pair of 8ft 6in (2.6m) diameter Stirling water tube boilers operating at 120psi replaced the Climax boilers: the Galloway boilers had already been removed. In 1924/5 motor-driven mechanical stokers were installed reducing the manpower requirements at the station.

The river outside the power station is still spanned by this narrow bridge which uses grooved tram rails as its main girders. This may be a survivor of a short wagonway used to bring coal across the river to feed the boilers (12 November 2017)

Despite both the hydro-electric and steam powered plant being superseded when the Manx Electric Railway started to draw its supply from the grid in 1935, both buildings are still standing. The main power station structure has been used as a film studio, but is now in industrial use, while the hydro-electric building appears to be used as a store by the local commissioners. The buildings' railway provenance is clear, as the economically-minded railway engineers made use of old rails for elements of the buildings. Outside the steam plant there is a small bridge across the Laxey River whose edge girders are formed tramway rails. The rails are of grooved street tramway rail rather than the flat bottom material generally used on the MER and may have been recovered from the Douglas horse tramway.

1930 was an unfortunate year for the MER with two major incidents in Laxey causing considerable damage to the tramway's infrastructure. On the night of Saturday and Sunday 5-6 April, a major fire at Laxey car shed resulted in the total loss of the building and many items of rolling stock (see page 10). The night of 17-18 September saw a second disaster strike Laxey when a major rainstorm in the north and centre of the island led to massive water flows down Laxey Glen and Glen Roy. The confluence of the rivers is by the Laxey Woollen Mill, about a quarter of a mile above the power station. The combined flow caused much structural damage to the village with flooding of Glen Road and the valley bottom. The bridge access to the Laxey power station (see pages 63 and 64) was destroyed and the plant itself rendered useless.

The weir which controlled the water flow to the MER's hydro-electric plant lies just downstream of the confluence and had silted up over the previous years. This was deemed to be the cause of the flood as a massive amount of debris accumulated behind the weir and diverted the river down Glen Road with consequential damage to adjoining properties.

Almost the end of the mercury arc rectifier's service at Laxey (see page 70), seen during an open day a month or so before decommissioning at the end of the 2013 season. The six anodes are located in the glowing tubes around the lower part of the bulb. Condensed mercury vapour can be seen running down the globe. The apparatus is about a metre tall (Sara Goodwins, 6 October 2013)

At the conclusion of a protracted legal case the MER was found wholly to blame for the flood, due to its failure to keep the river bed clear, and was found liable not only for the cost of damages to property along Glen Road but also the legal costs of the plaintiffs. Despite the severity of the flood the bridge, the Monks' Bridge, at Old Laxey survived the onslaught. Sadly, this historic bridge failed in a subsequent flood during the afternoon of 5 December 2015.

In the short term, the second generator set at Ballaglass was switched in to provide a substitute source of power. Ballaglass then supplied all the tramway's power requirements through the high-tension cabling, while Laxey power station was cleaned and its equipment dried out and repaired; restoration to full capability being achieved by late November 1930. Fortunately the loss of the power supply from the Laxey plant had not coincided with the peak holiday season, so although the flood had been traumatic, the effects on tramway operation and revenue were not as drastic as they might have been.

It is interesting to note that the transmission system used the high-tension AC system. During the clean-up operation, when the steam-powered generators at Laxey were not in use, the rotary converters were used in reverse mode, i.e., the DC supply from the hydro-electric plant or the batteries was inverted to transmit AC power along the line to Douglas, Groudle and Ballaglass. Ballaglass had not been re-equipped with alternators in 1903-4, so, for it to have been providing an AC supply to the remainder of the line, the rotary converters must also have been operating in reverse, i.e., they were being fed low voltage DC from the Ballaglass dynamos and transmitting high voltage AC. A reverse of the normal mode of operation, but perfectly possible, however not something that the author has seen mentioned previously.

The electricity supply on the island had taken major strides during the life of the tramway and, by the 1930s, a grid supply was widely available. On 7 November 1934 the MER agreed to switch to using the Manx Electricity Board's island grid, as this would be more economical. The MER's own plant could then be decommissioned. The scheme involved building a number of new substations which would take power directly from the grid at Ballaglass, Bellevue and Laxey all of which were fed at 33,000V, 50Hz. At Ballaglass the new equipment was housed in the old power station, while new brick buildings were provided at Bellevue and Laxey. The substations at Douglas, Groudle Glen and Snaefell were all fed with 6600V through the existing (1904) high-tension cabling from the Laxey transformer station. The standard equipment deployed was Hackbridge transformers coupled with Hewittic mercury-arc rectifiers. The ratings of the substations were: Douglas 200kW, Groudle 2x200kW, Laxey 2x200kW; Ballaglass 2x150kW; Bellevue 150kW and Snaefell 2x150kW. The new substation at Bellevue was located on the south side of the stop and was refurbished during the winter of 2016-7 (see page 16). The new substation at Laxey was built near the bridge over Lower Rencell Road on the Laxey side of the car shed (see page 15).

The two generator sets at Ballaglass ceased operation on 16 and 30 August 1934, but the building remained host to the 1934 substation equipment until 1989, when a new solid-state substation built into the abutment of the overbridge at nearby Ballagorry took over. Although the chimney has gone, the power station building survives, lying inland of the tramline a short distance on the Laxey side of the Ballaglass Glen stop and visible from passing trams. Its present day use is as a domestic residence, and one with a decidedly unusual character. The former coal store now houses an indoor swimming pool and this can be seen from the tramway through the skylights.

The steam plant at Laxey comprised four distinct sets of equipment as described earlier. The steam turbine (set 4) installed in 1920 was unused after 6 September 1934; set 3 (the Robb Armstrong unit) was not used after 22 September 1934 and the Bellis Morcom units, sets 1 and 2, were last used on 30 and 29 April 1935 respectively. The hydro-electric turbine was decommissioned after use on 28 April 1935. From 1 May 1935 the MER drew all power from the grid, and a chapter in the history of the tramway closed. Like many nationalized bodies the name of the supplier has varied over the years but it currently trades as The Manx Utilities Authority, a combined body for the island's water and electricity supplies.

The transmission of electrical power by high-tension AC is effective over large distances, but it needs to be converted to low voltage DC by substations near the point of use by the tramway. On the MER the substations are located about four miles apart: the closer the spacing the less the voltage drop, but the higher the capital and operational costs. Accordingly four miles seems to be a good compromise solution.

There has been a steady evolution in the transforming and rectification processes. Initially rotary converters were used. The most basic form is that the high voltage AC is first transformed to a lower voltage which supplies an alternating current motor mounted on the same shaft as a direct current generator which then feeds the local overhead. More efficient and compact rotary converters use a combination of AC and DC windings on the same armature so only one set of field coils is needed. Although the principles are simple, rotary convertors have drawbacks in that there are mechanical and electrical losses which appear as heat in the motor-generator set. In addition, maintenance of the relatively complex plant can be expensive and such equipment is now obsolete for traction purposes.

The next stage was the replacement of the rotary converters with more compact and electrically efficient mercury-arc rectifiers which have no large rotating masses to deal with. A mercury-arc rectifier has a pool of mercury, which acts as a cathode, at the bottom of a large glass bulb. For each phase of the input alternating current there is a pair of anodes, giving a total of six anodes, for the three-phase supply drawn from the island's grid. Mercury vapour only conducts electricity in one direction, due to the ionization of the mercury atoms. By centre tapping the secondary (i.e., low voltage) side of the transformer, each of the six anodes receives a positive voltage in sequence with its current flowing to the cathode through an arc. The electrical output through the cathode is direct current at an almost constant voltage, with a small ripple effect due to the multi-phase input. Heat generated by the current flow vaporizes the mercury which maintains the arc and its transmission of electricity. Mercury vapour condenses on the cool surface of the upper part if the bulb and drains back down to the cathodic pool. When operating a bright light is generated, the intensity of which is dependent on the amount of power being drawn. Cooling of the bulb is augmented by an electric fan.

The mercury-arc sets served the MER well over the years following their bulk installation in 1934-5 and it was only at the end of the 2017 season that the last set (at Groudle Glen) was switched out. This was probably one of the last in day-to-day use worldwide. In the latter half of the twentieth century solid-state rectification showed many benefits: such plant does not require manpower to be present while it is in operation and it can be controlled electronically from a remote location. As and when replacement equipment was required, the MER made the transition to solid-state technology. Semi-conductors, which only conduct electricty in one direction, such as silicon have replaced mercury vapour in transistor-based rectifiers. There are no moving parts in the equipment, power losses are low and reliability is high.

At present, substations are located at Derby Castle; Ballameanagh/Barroose (commissioned late 2017); near to Laxey Car Sheds (this installation replaced the nearby mercury-arc rectifier at the end of the 2013 season); The Bungalow (on the Snaefell Mountain Railway); Ballagorry (built into the infrastructure of the overbridge about half a mile south of the old power station at Ballaglass) and Bellevue, about two miles from Ramsey. The substation at Ballameanagh/Barroose (between Halfway and Baldrine) replaced the obsolete kit situated at Groudle Glen on private property near the viaduct. As the new supply at Ballameanagh is more centrally located between Derby Castle and Laxey it reduces the effects of voltage drop on the relatively long section between Groudle and Laxey.

Unusually the feed to the overhead at Ballagorry is not immediately next to the substation, but adjacent to the Ballagorry stop at pole 625. The line is on a steep gradient past the substation, so using the nearest pole, especially if the rails were wet, was not ideal for a section break where power should be shut off. Accordingly the feed was repositioned during 2014-5 to be at the top of the incline which is operationally more convenient.

THE TRAMWAY OVERHEAD

The tramway overhead is divided into sections which can be isolated from each other. In the event of any problems this enables a relatively short section to be isolated and worked on in safety whilst the remainder of the line is still operational. Feeder cables supply electricity to the overhead at the ends of each section. The feeders from the substations are carried along the line on the traction poles; these are the extra cables which are not used by the trams as contact wires and are supported on insulators on the poles themselves rather than from the bracket arms. When the pioneering tramway was constructed it did not follow the British Board of Trade regulations regarding section lengths: the technology preceded the regulations, which were not defined until after the tramway had reached Laxey. The section lengths between Douglas and Laxey were rather more than a mile each, with six sections in total. The subsequently-introduced UK regulations required maximum section lengths of half a mile, so the Ramsey extension had shorter sections which were typically rather more than half a mile as there is no mandatory requirement for the line to follow UK requirements. The present section lengths are greater than half a mile with feeder points more widely spaced. Unlike urban systems the MER never offered a highly-intensive service and it would be rare for several cars to be running in the same section with consequently high power demand, so the greater distance between feeder points mattered less.

The power supply to the sections along the line is controlled through knife switches located in cast iron section boxes which are generally positioned between the running lines adjacent to the traction poles carrying the feeder wires. Switchgear at the substations provides local feed direct to the overhead: in the case of Laxey, the feed cables are carried across the Glen Roy viaduct to the Snaefell Mountain overhead in Laxey station itself. Between sections there are short, around 12in (300mm), insulated (dead) lengths in the overhead. When crossing the dead lengths the motorman should shut off the tram's power by returning the controller handle to the off position. Failure to do so can lead to arcing as the full voltage comes into contact with the trolley wheel, which can cause burn damage to both the overhead and the tram's trolley wheel. Motormen are reminded of the need to coast under the section breaks as the pole-number labels on the feeder poles were given a red background when the labels were renewed during the winter of 2013-4. Feeder poles are generally on level, or nearly level, sections of track so that the temporary loss of power when coasting through the dead sections does not interrupt the smooth running of the tram. One feeder which needs careful attention is that at pole 811, just to the south of Lewaigue, which is close to both the stop and a level crossing. Heading south the tram has barely gained momentum when the controller must be set back to the off position to pass the feeder point. Power is re-applied as soon as possible for the long climb to Dreemskerry.

The section feeder box at Ballabeg carries the initials of the Isle of Man Tramways and Electric Power Company. The feeder cables on the traction pole can be isolated from the power supply by knife switches inside the box should it be necessary to isolate the overhead here. Knife switches have an insulated handle with a blade which is pivoted at its far end; when moved they move into or out of slots closing or opening the circuits (5 April 2015)

On straight track the overhead is positioned centrally over the running lines so that the lateral forces and any consequential wear on the trolley wheel and the wire are minimized. Central location of the wire is particularly desirable on the MER where fixed-head trolley poles are fitted, rather than the swivel heads common on the majority of trolley-pole equipped tramways. Swivel-head trolleys are designed to accommodate far larger lateral offsets between the track centre line and the overhead, with no wear or dewirement issues, but experience had shown them to be less suited to high-speed running.

With fixed-head trolleys, the wire on curves is offset to the inside of the curve: ideally the fixed trolley head should be tangential to the wire, minimizing lateral forces and the risk of dewirement. This arrangement satisfies the geometric requirements, where the car body is further round the curve than the trailing end of the trolley pole (see diagram).

Where there are crossovers between the two running lines a short length of a third wire is erected which enables the trolley wheel to follow the crossover through the pointwork without requiring guidance from the conductor. Guidance would be needed if frogs (in effect points in the overhead) were fitted. Typically the additional wire is tied back to the traction poles one and a half pole lengths

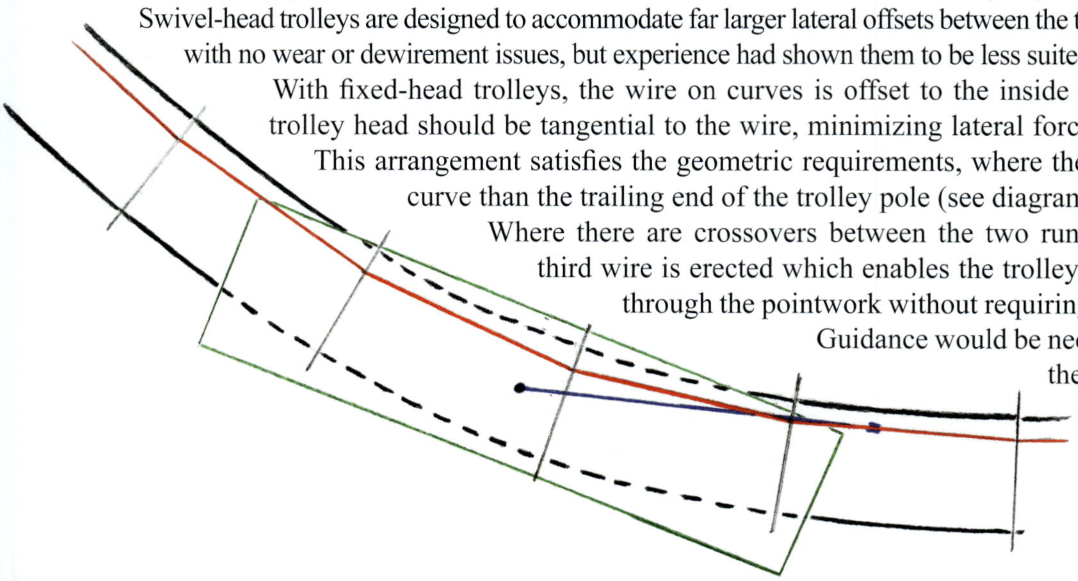

away from the centre of the crossover, coming close to the through running wires at the poles either side of the crossover, and following the track through the crossover. Using the crossover wires does, however, require the conductor to carry out a double de-poling exercise. In the past not all crossovers had the supplementary third wire and a different crossing-over technique was required. At these crossovers the car gained momentum before entering the crossover, then the motorman moved the controller to the off position; simultaneously the conductor pulled the trolley down from the overhead and held it down while the tram coasted across the crossover. The trolley pole was raised to the through wire when the other line was reached. The driver was notified that contact had been re-established, and that it was safe to move off, by bell signals from the conductor.

The crossover wire arrangement is clearly visible at Ballaragh as winter saloon 19 heads downhill towards Laxey. As the crossover wires are not joined to the running wires through frogs, de-poling is necessary to follow the wire. Power is supplied to the crossover wire by a connexion to the feeder running between the poles either side of the crossover. (25 October 2015)

On the Snaefell Mountain Railway, power is still supplied via Hopkinson bow collectors, just as it was when the line opened in 1895. The author believes that there are no other Hopkinson systems still in operation anywhere in the world, so this is an interesting line to observe in action. This overhead is designed so that as the wire sags between the support arms it will always be in contact with at least one of the two bow collectors located approximately above the bogies near the ends of each car. In the immediate vicinity of the support arms the bow collector loses contact, while that at the far end of the tram, remote from a support, remains in contact. To avoid the car losing contact with the overhead and becoming stranded (in the vernacular, 'stuck on the dead'), the support locations must be arranged so that it is not physically possible for a tram to be isolated from the overhead as it would be with both collectors below support points. Loss of power to a car would also de-activate its air compressor, impairing the reservoir pressure and one of the independent braking systems. However, as the pole spacing, even on sharp curves, is much greater than the length of the tram losing contact cannot happen.

Although not directly associated with the power supply, the rheostatic braking system on the Snaefell cars is worthy of mention. Since replacement of the cars' original motor bogies in 1975-6 by new bogies incorporating second-hand equipment from a batch of Aachen trams, normal braking on the Snaefell line has been provided by rheostatic braking. Electric current produced using the cars' motors acting as generators is dissipated as heat through banks of resistances added to the car roofs at the same time. The heat shimmer is particularly noticeable at Laxey Station whenever a descending car draws to a halt. The potential energy that the tram has gained by virtue of its elevation to the summit is converted during its descent; firstly into electrical energy through the car motors and then into heat in the resistances. Rheostatic braking has a major benefit in that it has an inbuilt anti-lock braking system: current generation only occurs when the wheels are turning the motors, so if a skid developed then the braking forces are instantly cut off and the skidding ceases. Conversely, rheostatic braking can never bring a tram to a complete halt but only reduce it to a slow steady pace. In addition, hand brakes acting on the wheel treads of the cars can be applied by separate brake wheels in the cabs. These provide braking on the non-Fell rail sections or bring the car to a stand once the car speed falls below that at which the rheostatic brakes are effective. They are also used as parking brakes. Wheel-tread brakes are not suitable for service braking on the mountain section due to the risk of wheel locking, especially on damp rails. An uncontrolled skid would be very dangerous and would cause wheel flats and damage to the rail running surface.

The ideal system would use the electricity generated by descending cars to power climbing cars, rather than dissipating it as heat in the resistances. In practice there are difficulties balancing supply with demand: some form of battery or capacitator storage would need to be added to the electrical supply system, together with suitably responsive control mechanism. Despite the evident attractions, electrical engineers have not yet developed a cost-effective way of achieving the goal of regenerative braking.

As the contact width of a bow collector is large, any crossover or branch wiring merely has to follow the approximate line of the track as the collector easily accommodates significant wire deviations from the track centre line. Crossover wires are not always needed. During the first part of the 2016 season single-line working was used between Laxey and The Bungalow with a temporary sluing of the track between the two lines on the level section at Lhergy Veg. No additional wiring needed to be installed as the bow collectors were always in contact with one of the two wires. At The Bungalow there are two crossovers, one either side of the mountain road crossing. The upper crossover is on practically level ground and no additional wiring is provided. The lower crossover lies on a slope: if an ascending car needs to use the crossover then loss of power would be unacceptable. Interestingly a third contact wire is supported parallel to those above the two tracks and supported by the adjacent traction poles, as opposed to following the line of the crossover track. Unusually a facing crossover is installed here: the standard practice is to use trailing crossovers so that accessing the wrong line requires a reversing manoeuvre, which is inherently safer.

The Hopkinson bow collectors are near the ends of the Snaefell cars. A metal hoop with a slightly concave top surface is supported by a sprung mechanism which adds resilience to the collector. When the cars were modified for rheostatic braking in the late 1970s banks of resisitors were added to the roof of the clerestory at the downhill end. Cars which can be used for the evening dining experience at the summit are fitted with roof mounted headlights as shown on car 3 (7 May 2003)

One advantage of the Hopkinson system is that the high cross winds sometimes encountered on the exposed upper parts of the Snaefell line cannot cause dewirements, which could be the case with a trolley-equipped system. Indeed this may be why the Hopkinson system has continued in use. As one of the bow collectors is always in contact with the overhead, power does not need be cut off when passing between sections as the two bow collectors are connected in parallel through the cars circuitry and hence at the same electric potential. The Hopkinson system requires the overhead to be supported so that loss of contact between a bow collector and the wire only occurs over short lengths close to the supports. This can only be achieved with accurate support heights, requiring more precision in maintaining the height of the overhead above the line than for alternative systems. Line ears

As Snaefell cars have bow collectors with a large side to side range the crossover wire configuration as seen directly above the 'No Public Right of Way' sign at The Bungalow does not need to follow the rails as is done on the MER. The crossover wire parallels the through wires and will pick up the bow collectors. (16 February 2016)

never come into contact with the collectors and are screw clamps. The overhead on the upper section of the line is removed over the winter, by releasing the screw clamps, as high winds, combined with the possible build up of ice on the wires, can lead to multiple breakages and collapse of the line. It is not unknown, but unfortunate, for a bout of extreme weather in early spring to damage the overhead after it has been re-installed for the summer season, leading to a delay in the start of services. Changes in temperature of the overhead cause the conductor wires to lengthen (hot weather) or contract (cold weather) with consequent changes in the wire sag between supports and the electrical contact between bow and wire. In practice this has little effect on the cars' operation.

An inescapable disadvantage of the Hopkinson system, in stark contrast with other collection systems, is that there is no quick and easy way to isolate the car from the overhead should this be needed in an emergency. A pantograph can be dropped using a driver-controlled switch and, of course, a trolley pole can be disengaged with a quick tug on the rope by the conductor.

The Manx Electric Railway also used the Hopkinson system at first, but this was replaced by the trolley wheel system after about four years. Although the Hopkinson system was installed for the initial line in 1893, and the Laxey extension in 1894, it was superseded by the now familiar trolley wheel system between Douglas and Laxey by the time the Ramsey extension opened in 1898-9. The existing motor cars were modified to the new system, as was the full length of the existing overhead between Douglas and Laxey. The Laxey to Ramsey extension has always operated on the trolley wheel system.

The electrical current collection system on the MER is unusual in a number of ways, and is still similar to that adopted in the late 1890s. Worldwide there has been a tendency to adopt pantograph current collectors, although there are still a few trolley-pole systems in use. The transition to pantographs has mainly been driven by the move to one-person operation of trams; the motorman is inevitably remote from the trolley rope, and pantographs cannot dewire. In contrast with the usual, though not exclusive, British practice, the MER continues to use fixed-head, as opposed to swivel-head, trolleys. Fixed-head systems have the disadvantage that the trolley wire, as noted above, needs to be more rigorously aligned relative to the track centre line than swivel-head systems, which accommodate greater lateral deviation between wire and track. Conversely the fixed head is simpler to manufacture and there is no swivel mechanism to maintain on the top of the trolleypoles.

The MER continues to use brass trolley wheels rather than the more usual carbon-insert slider heads. Carbon-insert sliding heads have a number of advantages, the principal one is that, being soft, the head, which is relatively inexpensive and easily replaceable, self-lubricates and wears preferentially, thus reducing wear on the overhead wires. In operation, carbon inserts are quieter than trolley wheels. Per car-mile carbon head inserts are cheaper than brass wheels and replacing them frequently is

Inset: a worn trolley wheel from an MER tram. The bottom of the groove has worn, distorting its width and there are signs of pitting from arc burns on the sides of the groove. Circumferential abrasions are also present from the axle mounting, but these are indistinct. Wheel diameter is 4in (105mm)

Left: emergency replacement of a worn trolley wheel is under way at Derby Castle using a white van as a mobile working platform. Car 1's pole has been swung round; its rope is held by an engineering team member on the right of the van, while a shiny new wheel is fitted by the high-visibility clad member of staff on the van's roof (5 April 2015)

generally more economical as overhead line life is extended. In service the carbon insert wears down and leaves greasy black deposits behind it, but examination of the roof of any tramcar will reveal dirt which has been dislodged by contact between the overhead and the collection device. In practice carbon insert heads are most beneficial on intensive services where the overhead becomes highly polished by the frequent passage of trams. The MER's relatively sparse service means that the economics are less crucial.

The small diameter of the MER trolley wheel means that it spins at a relatively high speed. Taking the contact diameter as 2.36in (60mm), and assuming no slippage, then over a single journey between Douglas and Ramsey the wheel rotates about 150,000 times, an at average speed in excess of 2000rpm, during the hour and a quarter journey. Abrasion occurs between the wheel and the axle on which it is mounted as well as in the groove where it contacts the overhead wire. In addition to the mechanical wear of the rolling surfaces there is continual burn damage to the surfaces of both the wheel and the wire due to electric arcing. Not surprisingly the useful life of a trolley wheel is relatively low. The rate of wear is dependent on the weather, and increases in wet or icy conditions. Replacement is usually necessary after around a week of normal use. Wear becomes apparent, both on and off the tram, by the generation of extraneous noise. On one occasion the author was aware of what sounded like a hammering noise coming from an adjacent traction pole, which was triggered by a badly worn trolley wheel wobbling on its axle on a tram over half a mile away, the noise growing louder as the tram neared. The crew had phoned for assistance and a new wheel was fitted on arrival at the terminus with only minor delays to the return service.

The MER also continues to use 'live' trolley poles, that is, they act as conductors for the electricity as well as carrying the trolley head. Normal practice elsewhere is that the pole is isolated from the collector and the electricity is carried to the controller by an insulated cable rather than through the pole itself. With a live pole, there is a potential danger that it may provide an electrical path between the wire and anything else it is simultaneously in contact with. An example might be that the trolley wheel is not located on the live wire but the pole rests against it and a higher part of the pole could contact a bracket arm, causing a traction pole to become live. This is unlikely in general but may happen if there is a dewirement.

PRACTICALITIES OF INSTALLATION

On the MER the overhead line is generally supported by traction poles situated between the running lines with lateral bracket arms reaching over both tracks. This practice differs from street tramways where the desirability of keeping the middle of the road free of poles - which present collision hazards to other road traffic - usually means that

Looking north, at the summit curve at Bulgham, there are a couple of extra poles on the outside of the curve. Pull-off wires and single curve suspensions hold the wires to a reasonably smooth curve. The large green pole on the top of the bank and the white box are part of a mobile phone installation and not MER property (26 September 2015)

side poles with span wires are used. On curved sections the overhead will tend to have relatively sharp kinks at the line ears with almost straight sectors between - so the wire line deviates from its ideal geometry. The length of the bracket arms varies on either sideof the centre poles: those supporting the wire on the outside of the curve being shorter than those supporting the wire on the side nearer the centre of curvature. This is due to the need to offset the wires towards the centre of curvature of the tracks. Curved line segments are not employed on the MER. Although these can reduce the likelihood of dewiring on sharp curves the extra cost, weight and complexity count against them. Again these are of most benefit on street systems where the higher cornering speeds that they allow assist traffic flow, especially at road junctions.

On a straight section of track, with well-installed overhead, the traction poles will be supporting only vertical loads - the weight of the wires and arms - except when there is significant drag loading from high cross winds. On curves, the tension in the overhead pulls the top of the traction pole towards the centre of curvature, inducing lateral bending in the pole. Poles on curves are installed with a slight outwards lean, so that under the tension loads, they will bend to be nearly vertical. On sharp curves, with the centre pole system, the bending forces are larger and, in some cases, the traction poles in these locations are of a stiffer and stronger section rather than the standard poles used on straight track. The stiffer poles may be similar to the standard ones, but of increased diameter, or they may be fabricated by welding three different diameter pipe sections together in a 'telescope' formation.

On tighter curves, the poles are more closely spaced than on straight track in order to keep the wire sufficiently close to the ideal geometry. On some of the more extreme curves on the tramway, the centre pole system is adapted or abandoned entirely, and a more complex catenary system is employed where a number of poles are positioned to either side of the tracks and support the twin overhead lines by a network of tensioned cables. Such systems can be observed at several points along the line, for example: near Howstrake; across the Groudle Glen Viaduct; at the Halfway road crossing; just south of Garwick Glen; the Ballabeg road crossing; across Mines Road at Laxey, and the corner at Bulgham Head (see photograph page 75). Such 'knitting' is relatively complex as each segment of support wire needs to be correctly tensioned in order to pull and hold the smooth geometric curve for the contact wires around the bend. Damage due to de-poling, or for other reasons, is more difficult to attend to than on plain line sections, and care is needed by motormen when negotiating the catenary sections. Due to the tight curvature where such systems are used, the tram speed is, of course, likely to be relatively low. Once again the poles placed to the side of the line are supporting not only the weight of the overhead, but are also being bent towards the track centre line due to the tension in the pull-off wires that maintain the contact wire geometry. Accordingly the poles should be installed with an outward lean so that, under load, they bend to be nearly vertical.

Along Walpole Road, on the approach to Ramsey, the wires for both tracks are supported by long bracket arms from poles placed on the inland side of the line, so that the space between the tracks is clear. When the tramway was authorized, Ramsey Town Commissioners had planned to pave the width of the street,

In Walpole Road, Ramsey, long-length side bracket arms cantilever over both tracks. The bracket arms are supported by two stay wires to reduce their tendency to sag under the weight of the wires. Winter saloon 20 and trailer 41 join Walpole Road as they near the end of their trip to Ramsey (30 August 2015)

This traction pole carries two different forms of overhead. On the left is the visibly heavier grooved wire, with a short line ear fitting into the groove, and with bellows-shaped black insulators to the span wire. On the right, the older, lighter, round wire is gripped on its sides by a long line ear insulated by ceramic globes. Turnbuckles near the traction pole allow tensioning of the span wires. Stay wires tie the bracket arms to the top of the pole. The power feeder wire, with a vertically-mounted insulator, is carried at the top of the pole, which is capped with a finial to prevent water ingress. The bracket arms and their finials differ, with the newer design on the left (21 February 2018)

which would have given the MER its only length of street running track (see page 37). Paving never took place, but the unusual support of the overhead is still maintained, although the original Victorian decorative iron scrollwork disappeared, during the early years of the twenty-first century, when the poles were replaced. With their long side arms these poles carry asymmetric loads and have high lateral bending forces at their bases. In order to cater for the greater bending forces the poles on this section of the line are of greater diameter than the standard centre poles. There are also a few long bracket arms at Laxey, which support the overhead for both lines, near the Mines Road crossing. These were erected over the winter of 2013-4 when new track, incorporating a crossover, was laid there as part of the Laxey Station redevelopment scheme. Such poles should be installed with an outward lean so that the bending loads from the weight of the wires and bracket arms pull them to be nearly vertical.

In order to power the trams the overhead line is supplied with electricity at a positive voltage of 500. To do this the wire must be held by, but electrically insulated from, the supporting infrastructure. Leakage of electricity is impossible to prevent in its entirety, however the design of the overhead aims to inhibit this as far as is practical. Steel is the most economical and durable material for traction poles, bracket arms and stays, but is a good conductor of electricity and will provide a path to earth for any stray electricity as the base of the pole is buried and probably damp. The bracket arms are held horizontal by the bracing stay wires, which are under tension; both are separately clamped to the upper part of the traction pole. The span wire is tensioned by a turnbuckle so that the hanger is laterally restrained but retains a small amount of vertical flexibility. The contact wire is isolated from the steel components on either side by insulators in line with the hanger. As noted below the line ears vary in their design and weight depending on the wire section in use.

Above: tensioning the new grooved wire is essential and this arrangement at Onchan Head shows one way of stressing the wire. The top of the contact wire is gripped by a clamp. Two insulators isolate the steel cable from the line voltage. The cable is tensioned back to the next traction pole (9 April 2015)

Where the new grooved-section wire is deployed its higher tension needs to be resisted. One approach is to transfer the load to a steel cable which is tied off at mid-height on the next pole. In this case the top of the pole behind the photographer is connected to the mid point of the former Marine Drive pole via a clamp. Both techniques reduce the bending loads at the base of the traction pole at the end of the high tension section (9 February 2019)

When the line was built the original trolley wire was hard-drawn copper wire to American Wire Gauge (AWG) 'O' section, nominal diameter 0.325 inches (8.26mm). This was supplied in either mile or half mile lengths and weighed about 320lb per 1000ft (475kg/km). The recommended tension for this section is 750lbf (340kg), although it had not been the practice to tension specifically to this level on the MER.

The MER is switching to using heavier section overhead wire which is being deployed as the smaller section wires become life expired and need replacement. The new wire has a cross-sectional area of 0.17in^2 (107mm^2) and a weight of 640lb per 1000ft (952kg/km), double that of the older wire. The heavier-section line has a number of advantages. It has lower electrical power losses due to its greater cross-sectional area and electrical conductivity, and it is stronger. During installation the wire is put into higher tension, typically 800lbf (400kg), to reduce sagging between traction poles under its greater weight. The overhead must form a dynamically stable system, when the trolley wheel running along the wire applies moving contact forces: under the same tension the heavier wire has a lower natural frequency than the lighter wire, which could lead to excessively large oscillations and hence damage. Higher operating speeds require higher tensions and the oscillation problem is avoided by applying a tension which would be adequate for speeds greater than those attained in operation. A disadvantage of the highly-stressed wire is that, if it breaks, the effect can be like releasing a spring: the energy stored in the wire is released and can twist the bracket arms over a significant number of spans. Where the heavier-section wire comes to an end, the normal procedure is to take the tension in the wire to the next traction pole, securing it at about half height, so that the wire tension does not generate excessive bending in the pole where it is tied off. The extra stay wire may connect the top of one pole to a clamp at half height on the next so that the overhead tension forces are split between the poles.

Above: the final few metres of new overhead line are seen on a cable drum at Laxey. The wire has a cross-sectional area of 0.17in^2 (107mm^2) and is made by a hard drawing process, the work-hardening leading to enhanced strength (5 July 2017)

Left: a close up shows the form of the grooved wire. Overhead line wire is primarily copper which is an excellent conductor of electricity. On the head there are identification grooves. A central groove indicates pure copper; an offset groove indicates 0.4% tin content and twin grooves, as here, 0.1% silver content (5 July 2017)

A twin grip wire hanger near Ballaskeig. Although the hanger itself is brand new it is suspended from one of the 'Aetna' brand items which date from the initial installation of the overhead in Victorian days. An interesting mix of technology (28 February 2018)

The heavier wire comes in a figure-of-eight section so that the line ears only grip the top section, leaving the lower part to interact with the trolley wheels. The older wire is of round section with the line ears gripping the sides of the wire: the ears come into contact with the passing trolley wheels of the trams. This causes more noise, and the repeated impact can lead to damage to both the line ears and trolley wheels. The line ears for the heavier section grip a shorter length of wire than the round wire. Recently some wire has been suspended using twin grip brackets, where the distance between the pair of grips is about 12in (300mm). The more complex design of hanger reduces the localized flexure of the wire during the passage of the trolley wheel, leading to lower stresses and reduced risk of fatigue failure.

With the passage of each tramcar, the upward force from the sprung trolley base causes the contact wire to be bent upwards in the vertical plane. The clamping effect of the line ears gives stress concentrations at the edges of each ear with high local bending stresses induced in the wire. This creates a fatigue hot spot, so failure of the wire in service usually occurs at the edge of an ear. The upward pressure of the trolley wheel on the wire creates a bow wave in the overhead which precedes the tram. This means that wire fatigue failure can occur in front of a tram. The unexpected appearance of a live wire snaking down in front of the cab requires quick reactions from the motorman.

An inescapable feature of the Manx Electric Railway is the long line of traction poles which support the overhead. In general the poles are numbered in sequence from 1, at Derby Castle, through to 903 at the end of the line in Ramsey Plaza station, although there are rather more than this many poles in total. In places, such as between Eskadale and Halfway, additional centre poles have been added to ensure that the overhead has a smoother curve in plan, allowing a higher speed with a reduced risk of de-poling than otherwise possible. Where there are side poles with pull-off wires the assignment of numbers is even more complex. Poles with numbers such as 174A or 245B mean that no simple

Above: the feeder pole at Braeside, on King Edward Road, is doing a lot of work. Not only does it carry the running wire, but also the power-cable feeds to sections of both lines either side of the pole. Separating the sections are insulated line ears. In addition there are feeds from the central wire between the tracks, which carries power to other sections. The pole also carries one of the old-style stop flags (Sara Goodwins 13 May 2012)

Left: the sharp S bend at Ballaglass is one where higher-strength fabricated traction poles are deployed, because of the higher bending loads due to the wire geometry. These are easily identified by the step changes in section rather than the tapered changes found on the standard poles. Open motor 32 and trailer 62 are heading south (1 April 2018)

Adjacent to the siding at Dhoon Quarry is pole 558A which, unusually for the MER, is made of wood rather than steel. It carries a single bracket arm carrying the wire over the siding. The upper section of the Snaefell line still employs several wooden poles (29 July 2017)

count is possible. Adding in the supplementary supports in the vicinity of the car sheds and at Dhoon Quarry, the number of traction poles on the MER is closer to a thousand. Revisions to the overhead occur from time to time, with poles added or removed, which will amend the total in use.

The Snaefell Mountain Railway has its own pole numbering system, starting at 1000 in Laxey Station and working its way to the summit. A few supplementary poles in the area of the depot above Laxey, and at The Bungalow, add around two hundred to the MER total, with the pole immediately before the point at the summit being numbered 1185. In general, the traction poles are of tubular steel with a stepped section giving a greater bending moment capacity in the lower part of the pole, where the loads peak at the point where the pole is set in concrete. There is a number of wooden poles on the mountain section and at least one wooden pole, located in Dhoon Quarry sidings, on the MER. The numbering of the poles allows tram crews to give an accurate report to the engineering team of the location of any observed defects along the line. All poles are labelled with plastic tags and white lettering. The standard background is dark blue, but every twentieth pole has a bright green background and electrical feeder poles have a red background.

The traction poles are inevitably in exposed locations and, along the MER, they are rarely far from the sea. Wind-borne salty sea spray provides an ideal environment for corrosion, with the consequent requirements for maintenance and replacement of life-expired poles. Galvanized steel poles, which have been dipped in molten zinc to provide a corrosion resistant finish, do not need painting and are now used to replace old poles. The galvanized poles are starker in appearance than the traditional green-painted poles. Not surprisingly, older poles, suffering from various degrees of corrosion and coating loss are evident along the line. Strengthening of poles can be effected by filling them with concrete and adding steel reinforcement to the mix. Examination of the line shows that, in some locations, there are one or sometimes two stumps of removed poles adjacent to the present incumbent: the presence of the end of a recycled fishplate in the stump indicates the re-use of surplus scrap steel instead of new reinforcement bars before concrete filler has been added. The painting of non-galvanized poles is a time consuming exercise and has little effect at the critical section which is where the pole enters the ground. At that point the pole is most likely to be damp, corroded and most highly stressed.

Especially noteworthy are the traction poles taken from the former Douglas Southern Electric Tramway, also known as the Marine Drive Tramway, which ran between Douglas Head and Port Soderick. These are distinctive and easily recognisable by the cast collars at their change of cross-section (see standing pole in the foreground of photograph on opposite page). They were supplied by Morris Tasker and Co., of Philadelphia and made of high grade steel with the top sections galvanized. The line opened in 1896 and the poles were acquired at a bargain price by the MER, after closure of the Marine Drive Tramway following the Second World War. (Strictly speaking, the Marine Drive Tramway was not formally closed but, having ceased operation shortly after the outbreak of war in 1939, it was deemed uneconomic to repair after the end of hostilities and it never re-opened.) These second-hand poles still appear to be in remarkably good condition considering their age and exposure to the weather. They have proved a good investment, if not for the Douglas Southern, then certainly for the MER, which has used them for far longer than their original purchaser.

When the first part of the line was constructed there were few tramway installations in the British Isles, so much of the equipment was imported from the United States, originating from the plant of Albert and J.M. Anderson of Boston, Massachusetts and carrying their 'Aetna' brand name (see caption on bottom photograph page 78). That some of these fittings, insulators and line ears, may still be seen along the line speaks well of their quality and durability. The age of the overhead fittings varies considerably along the line and depends on the repair and renewal history of each section. The original insulators were of ceramic materials and could be in various forms. Typical of these is a ceramic globe with fixing loops cast in, but later a loop design accommodated two strands of wire passed through a block of material. More recently, insulating materials of heavy-duty plastic with a bellows-like appearance have superseded many of the older fittings. All replacements are now made with this design of insulator supported on galvanised bracket arms, and brought to site as pre-assembled units. When a length of contact wire is renewed, the current practice is to replace the run of bracket arms with new ones with short line ears (see top photograph page 77) over the whole length which is receiving the grooved wire, typically about half a mile. This is normally done over the winter closed period, when sections of the tramway can be denuded of overhead for several weeks following removal of the old fittings and before the new are installed. Typically two or three such lengths are replaced each winter: priority is usually given to areas where track renewal is also taking place, as removing the overhead gives easier works access for the mechanical plant - cranes and diggers - used for ballast and track component removal and replacement.

Inevitably the overhead gets wet and, on the more exposed coastal sections of line, there is an ever present risk of salt spray being blown onto the wires. Dissolved salts are an excellent electrolyte, i.e. they conduct electricty, and the potential for leakage to earth across damp insulators cannot be eliminated. If the insulation breaks down then there is a risk of the insulator burning out. Stray currents through the ground can cause electrolytic action on buried services such as metal pipes and lead to their rapid corrosion. This problem was discovered very early on in the operation of electric tramways. In some early installations in the United States, the overhead was energized at a negative potential and the earth return was positive: some buried pipes in the vicinity of the earth return dissolved in a matter of months. From the point of view of the physics it is the voltage difference, of either polarity, which drives the traction motors, but the side effects were drastic. Checks are made on a regular basis of the magnitude of the earth leakage current from each substation. When high leakage is observed the overhead crew need to locate the problem, which means walking the line. They look for evidence of burnt-out insulators and test the voltage difference between each pole and earth. An unresolved problem means that there is a danger that a pedestrian or animal might come into contact with a live pole and receive a shock: this is unlikely to be fatal but would be unpleasant.

Trees brought down by strong winds can affect the overhead installation. A few poles south of Ballig a tall fir tree fell across the A2 road and landed on the wires. The resulting increased tension in the wires pulled pole 592 towards the centre of curvature of the track and the rusted section below the ballast failed with this spectacular effect. The main road was quickly cleared by the Highways Authority, but as the pole tumbled during the winter closed season, the engineers' presence is not immediately required (Sara Goodwins 16 December 2018)

The electrical overhead of tramways has always been susceptible to lightning strike: the metal poles pointing to the sky suspending high-conductivity copper wires above open country are an obvious attraction for electrical discharges. The power of a high voltage strike can prove very destructive to the insulators on an affected section. As an example, a major storm near the end of the 2017 operating season caused major damage to one of the sections of the MER overhead, between Groudle Glen and Halfway. Many of the insulators were damaged between two feeder points, and major earth leakage problems were apparent. Fortunately the overhead on the other track was unaffected and single-line working was instituted while the damaged section was inspected and insulators replaced. Also, fortunately the storm was at night and no trams were running or affected by the voltage surge. Clearly there is no way to protect the overhead from lightning strike and any attempt to design it to such a high standard as to resist strikes would be grossly uneconomic.

Maintaining the overhead and electricity supply of the MER and SMR has seen a continual process of modernization and improvement over the past century and a quarter. Although the basic principles are unchanged, and the appearance of the installations little changed, the technology keeping the cars running is up to twenty-first century standards.

CHAPTER 5

MAINTENANCE, LOGISTICS & VISITING VEHICLES

The logistics of maintaining the Manx Electric Railway and the Snaefell Mountain Railway show major differences between the early days of the lines and the present day. Indeed, there have been significant changes between the processes employed twenty years ago and those of today. The driving forces for change are the decrease in the availability, and the consequent increase in cost, of ready manual labour, and the progressive move to mechanization of maintenance tasks. Society's attitudes to health and safety have also evolved and more structured ways of working have been implemented.

There are only two practical ways to access a railway line for maintenance: men and materials can be brought to site by railed vehicles along the line, or local access from neighbouring roads is required. Access by helicopter is too expensive. With time there has been a slow, but steady, change from predominantly rail-based working, to a far greater use of road vehicles. Concurrently there has been a shift from direct labour, to the use of external contractors, many of whom have neither ready access to railway motive power nor rail wagons for carrying materials and equipment.

Bags of ballast have been unloaded from the Isle of Man Railways' road lorry at Dreemskerry. The straps of a bag are being looped over the tines on a bucket of a JCB, which is ferrying bags downhill where extra ballast is being placed (7 January 2016)

Having been borrowed from the steam railway a ballast hopper wagon is unloaded from a low loader in Ramsey Station prior to the major bridge repair works at Ballure over the winter of 2014-5. Note the special unloading ramp rails: the wagon is about to be winched down to the track. When being moved by road the wagon is strapped down to the rails on the low-loader (2 November 2014)

In common with most tramway systems, the MER assigns particular fleet members to the engineering team. Typically these would have been the older motor cars and, indeed, in the 1950s and 1960s both cars 1 and 2 were often dedicated to works duties (see title page). Photographs of these original cars carrying ladders suspended on hooks from the underframe are well known. To offer crews some protection from the ravages of the Manx weather, some home made plastic windscreens were added to the old trams. They were not the most aesthetically pleasing modification but still very welcome, if rudimentary, protection from the cold winter wind and rain. There are two points of view on the use of these historic cars in this way: the purist will claim that this was an abuse of items of great industrial archaeological interest, but the realist will acknowledge that their continued use led to their eventual preservation and restoration to the cherished cars that they are today.

Well into the 1990s engineers' cars appeared out and about on the line, in between the service cars. Their disparate duties included carrying track components and tools to site in open wagons; delivery of rails on bogie flat trucks from the various stockpiles held around the system; taking ballast to site in hopper wagons; spraying weedkiller along the line, and moving the tower wagon to sites where attention to the overhead line was needed. At that time there were

Early in the morning car 33 is propelling the wire car, number 52, wrong line on the descent from Howstrake towards Groudle Glen. Because his view of the track is obstructed the motorman is being guided by hand signals from his colleague. The wire crew has probably attended to a minor fault between here and Onchan Head and is returning to base at Laxey. The first service car will be along in about an hour, by which time 33 and 52 will be out of the way (29 July 2015)

rather more crossovers on the MER than now, so that it was relatively easy for a works car and wagon to be shunted out of the way by a short excursion to the nearest crossover when a service car was due. Nifty working by the crews kept the working time to a maximum, while minimizing delays to the service. With more crossovers any single-line working could be restricted to shorter line lengths, when required, with less disruption to the service. The reduction in the number of crossovers over time is perhaps a reflexion of the changed working methods.

Historically there were no qualms about overhead line crews working on live overhead. The contact wire may have been at working voltage (500V), but, with a wooden tower wagon, rubber gloves and rubber soled boots, the possibility of the crew providing a path to earth was deemed remote. Modern health and safety requirements mean that work on the overhead should now only take place on a section that is electrically isolated. The practicalities of shunting the tower wagon during normal service have therefore been reduced as any motor car would, of necessity, be isolated from the electricity supply while work was taking place.

Left: as it is Sunday, no relaying work is under way today. The contractor's locomotive, the now anonymous Pig, *and wagon are parked at Lewaigue, near the materials storage compound, which is behind the hedge on the left. Single-line working is in operation on the other track. The Lewaigue crossover is behind the photographer, with enough room for a tram and trailer to draw up before reversing to the nearer line (18 June 2017)*

Below: RMS Locotec's Ruston and Hornsby 0-6-0 diesel H048 Bertie *is parked in the MER siding adjacent to Mines Road in Laxey. Relaying work is under way between here and Minorca with the land side track having been removed.* Bertie *will have been busy during the day on the remaining track, delivering materials and removing scrap (5 May 2008)*

Below: diesel-electric locomotive 34 on test in Laxey station. Gleaming in its new yellow paint, number 34 has shunted the new wire car built on the underframe of trailer 52 into the goods shed. The motorman clutches the controller handles as he edges past the generator heading for the nearer cab (9 May 2008)

Locomotive number 23, stored without trucks, on the concrete hard standing at the back of Laxey car shed. This is the only officially named item of rolling stock on the MER. The cast nameplates Dr R. Preston Hendry *are carried on the boards above the cab doors. These commemorate an avid supporter of the MER. On the right is freight trailer 26, formerly passenger car 10. The bodywork of the four cars 10-12 was identical to those of the six Snaefell cars delivered at the same time in 1895. Number 10 was converted in 1918 (24 September 2015)*

One of the advantages of the narrow-gauge track used by the MER is that a wide range of road vehicles can be driven along the line with their road wheels running on the sleeper ends, outside the track gauge. There is a minor risk that the rail fixings may be damaged by this process, but it is not unusual for maintenance vehicles to be used in this way. One example would be the use of a cherry-picker to give access to the overhead for attention to a line ear or other defective component (see page 96). Nowadays, the normal technique for placing ballast is for a number of large bags, each containing around 16cwt (850kg), to be delivered by road lorry to an adjacent level crossing. The ballast is then drawn to the site on a wagon hauled by an industrial diesel locomotive. Bags of ballast may also be carried along the line using a lifting hook on the front of a standard JCB type of digger. The bags are then split and the stones distributed when the site is reached. For longer lengths of ballasting the MER borrows a hopper wagon from the Isle of Man Railway. Typically this is brought to the line by a low loader lorry and unloaded directly onto the tracks via a ramp.

The end dash panel identifies trailer 45. To give an add-itional flat wagon for works duties the body was removed. The vehicle retains the hand brake wheel at one end: it is hidden from view by the dash panel. Number 45 is parked outside Laxey car shed, a not uncommon occurrence when it was not in use (9 May 2007)

A tractor is often used in place of a motor car to move the tower wagon/wire car along the line by attaching a towbar to the railway coupling. This is particularly useful when a length of line is being worked on with the power switched off, or when a long length of overhead wire is being installed. The wire car is brought to site by the tram allocated to the wire crew for the purpose. The tram is parked near the site while the power is switched off.

At the time of writing, the engineers usually employ open motor car 33 as their workhorse. This car is normally stabled in Laxey shed, along with the wire car, number 52, so that, when required, the pair may be dispatched towards either end of the line. Car 33 is, however, made available for traffic use when required, particularly during the TT race period, the enthusiast events of 'Rush Hour on The Railways' and the Manx Transport Heritage Festival, when practically all serviceable rolling stock is called on to handle the crowds with intensive services.

Using tractors to bring hedge cutting and grass trimming equipment for lineside tidying is another use of mechanical equipment which allows one man to clear a considerable length of encroaching undergrowth with ease. Local clearance of weeds and the like, particularly near the stops, is handled by a crew in a pickup truck arriving with hand held strimmers and hedge cutters for a session of 'gardening' activity when required. This usually happens when a normal service is operating and, as the noise of the equipment can mask the sound of approaching trams, a lookout may be posted.

Above: prior to the modification of number 52, the MER tower wagon facilities were more primitive. By the feeder pole at Bulgham summit corner, an older tower wagon is shepherded by car 7, as the service car passes by on the other line. Note that the overhead line crew accessed the working area by scaling a near vertical frame. In inclement weather, particularly with tools, this cannot have been an easy task (10 May 2002)

Right: clearing the undergrowth is taking place on the landside line near Minorca. The tractor carries a flail cutter on the yellow arm visible behind the cab. Typically a couple of passes are made with swathes cut through at different levels to clear the lineside. Meanwhile a southbound service car proceeds past with caution. Moving the tractor to allow trams to pass is no problem (31 July 2015)

Diesel-electric locomotive 34 seen from the trailer of a service car, with the wire car, number 52, near Queen's Drive in Ramsey. The bracket arm is on the ground and the wire is sagging, so the crew are almost certainly about to fit a replacement overhead support to allow normal service to recommence (28 May 2014)

All of these tasks are examples of the increased use of mechanical assistance. In earlier days the control of lineside vegetation was handled by hand tools and required a significant number of men to keep the eighteen-mile line clear. Historic photographs from the 1950s often show weed-strewn tracks where the vegetation control was neglected due to the parlous financial state of the MER in its final years before nationalization in 1957. Weeds need to be kept down on the running line as root growth can lead to the ballast becoming clogged. Drainage is impaired and the moist conditions can accelerate rotting of sleepers. Weedkiller can be applied from road vehicles or by personnel with hand sprays fed from backpacks for localized areas.

Wagon 21 in Laxey shed, as originally constructed with dropsides, ideal for carrying stone from the quarries, but with plenty of capacity for other duties when required (Courtesy, Travel Lens Photographic 1951)

Wagon 21 has appeared in a number of guises since it first entered service as an open wagon. Between 2000 and 2008 it was fitted with this hopper arrangement. Ballast discharge is controlled by handwheels on the far side of the body: each hopper delivered ballast to one side of the track. Loading was by mechanical diggers scooping up ballast from the stockpile at Dhoon Quarry, where the wagon is in the siding (8 May 2007)

Wagon 21 is again parked in the Dhoon Quarry siding but the hoppers have been removed and it has reverted to being a flat wagon. It is carrying a light load of a few pieces of timber. Interestingly, since the date of the previous photograph, this vehicle has acquired piping connexions for air brakes: the brake cylinder is visible suspended beneath the centre of the wagon (2 February 2014)

It is unusual to see the Wickham Railcar and trailer in motion, but early one morning in the closed season it was caught on camera heading towards Laxey shortly after the summit curve at Bulgham. The trailer is carrying a collection of traffic cones and traffic barriers, so it is likely that these have been recovered from a works site at a level crossing. The end windscreens provide scant protection from the weather, but the crew seem comfortable enough (26 February 2018)

Permanent way programmes on the MER have often brought hired diesel locomotives to the line. A frequent source of motive power has been the Bord na Mona in Eire, where the locomotives previously handled wagonloads of peat extracted from the bogs in the centre of Ireland. They ran on lightly laid track, installed to the Irish narrow gauge of 3'-0", identical to that used by the Isle of Man. Since 2008 the 0-4-0 diesel, *Pig*, has been a long term visitor to the Isle of Man. Built by Motor-Rail in 1980, *Pig* was purchased by RMS Locotec from Bord na Mona in August 2008, and spent the next two years on Manx permanent way duties. Taken back to the Weardale Railway (County Durham), where industrial locomotive hire specialists RMS Locotec are based, between 2010 and 2014, *Pig* returned in 2014 and has worked on both the Manx Electric and Isle of Man Steam Railways, largely on work carried out by Manx Rail Projects of Laxey. *Pig* was often parked in the siding at Dhoon Quarry. However, Manx Rail Projects ceased trading in late 2016, and *Pig* has latterly been in the care of island-based contractor Auldyn Construction. The locomotive has been repainted in a yellow ochre livery and, having lost its cast nameplate, is now anonymous (see top photograph on page 84). The locomotive appears from time to time on the MER, and also the steam railway, being brought to site by lorry. It was used on the MER during the 2017 relay of part of the land-side line between Lewaigue and Bellevue. Materials were brought to site from Lewaigue using *Pig* and a small truck. *Pig* has since appeared in 2018 on the track relay work between Dhoon Quarry and Glen Mona.

In 2006-10 a more powerful permanent way locomotive, supplied by RMS Locotec, was *Bertie*, a Ruston and Hornsby 0-6-0 diesel shunter, built in 1949 and numbered H048. Initially it was stabled at Laxey in the remains of the, by then roofless, second Laxey car shed. When the Laxey shed was being rebuilt *Bertie* was more likely to be seen in the siding at Dumbell's Row (see middle photograph on page 84).

Specialized Rolling Stock

Early in the twenty-first century the Manx Electric Railway converted the former Snaefell Mountain Railway replica goods tram, Number 7, (*Maria*) to be a self-propelled maintenance vehicle. The conversion work was started in 2003 but the locomotive was rarely used before 2008. A standard pair of electric motor bogies was supplied from car 25, and a diesel-engine-driven generator installed on the underframe, in effect converting the vehicle to a diesel-electric locomotive. Carrying the number 34, and painted in a bright yellow livery with bold red stripes on the cab ends (see page 84), this locomotive has seen use in maintaining and installing new overhead wiring, and also hauling engineering wagons during the winter season. At the time of writing, the locomotive has been out of use since early

Right: the three tipper wagons which originated on the Lochaber Narrow Gauge Railway in Scotland were last used in 2009. They have spent the majority of the time since in the stub siding in the old loading dock at Dhoon Quarry. When the Dhoon West Quarry was active, a narrow gauge line passed under the main coast road and ended at the stone crushing plant near here. Wagons were loaded here for onward transmission (26 September 2015)

Below: the headshunt outside Laxey car shed is often used to park little-used wagons. One of the three tipper wagons, which arrived on the MER in 1997, is joined by open wagon 8. The tipper's paintwork is in good condition as it is a recent arrival. Open wagon 8 has since been fully restored, and makes appearances during enthusiast events and photographic charters, demonstrating what an MER freight service used to look like (9 May 2000)

2016, and it is not known when this versatile vehicle will return to engineering duties. Maintenance of number 34 has been complicated by its unique configuration.

This is not the first time that the MER has had its own locomotive: number 23 was a steeple-cabbed electric locomotive built by the Isle of Man Tramways and Electric Power Company in 1900 for freight duties. Unfortunately it was damaged in an accident in 1914. It remained stored until it reappeared in 1925, on a new underframe with two six-ton wagon bodies flanking the central cab unit, and saw use until 1944. At the time of writing, this interesting vehicle is stored in Laxey Car Shed, without trucks (see photograph on page 85). Although locomotive 23 was never a dedicated engineers' locomotive, it seems likely that it could have proved useful in this sphere.

There are a number of other specialized items of rolling stock on the MER dedicated to engineering use. These cover a wide range of purposes: overhead maintenance; carriage of track components to and from site; placing of ballast on the line; movement of personnel and clearance of organic rubbish. Some tasks, such as spraying weedkiller on the track bed, are no longer carried out from engineering rolling stock but by road vehicles, or on foot.

One of the most important engineering vehicles is the wire car and tower wagon, number 52 (see photograph on page 87). This is built on the underframe of one of the early (1893) passenger trailers. Its body and seats were removed during the winter months but it was restored for passenger use each summer. However, from 1951 it remained as a permanent-way flat car, retaining only the Douglas end dash panel. The present superstructure was constructed in 2008, and the vehicle replaced the previous, more basic, tower wagons which comprised either wooden lattice towers on 4-wheel wagon underframes, or a converted van. The main feature of No 52 is that the working platform, which is surrounded by a stout wooden safety frame, is mounted on a scissors mechanism so that personnel and equipment may be loaded at a low level and the platform raised to the working height. At the Douglas end of the car a pair of trunnions carries a horizontal axle, on which a drum of overhead wire may be loaded, facilitating the unreeling of replacement power cable when required. As noted above (see photograph on page 83) this versatile vehicle is normally stabled in Laxey car shed and commonly paired with open motor car 33.

A couple of flat wagons are available for general use. Former passenger trailer number 45 (see photograph on page 85) had its body removed in 2004 in order to provide additional rolling stock for major track relaying programs. At the time this was stated to be a temporary measure, but regrettably it seems that the trailer will not be returned to passenger use. Between 2004 and 2017 number 45 was most commonly to be found in the headshunt outside Laxey car shed, although it was moved to the siding at Dhoon Quarry early in 2018 and has seen little, if any, use since.

Right: immediately before the 2018 Christmas holidays, there was a gathering of equipment at Dhoon Quarry ready for work in the New Year. In the Dhoon Quarry siding a Simplex diesel locomotive has been borrowed from the Isle of Man Railway. Looking a bit careworn the locomotive sports the owner's ornate crest on the cabside (20 December 2018)

Below: Isle of Man Railway well wagon number 2 has also been borrowed. The frame, fabricated from welded channel sections, is considerably more modern than the axle boxes which bear IMR initials and were presumably salvaged from an older vehicle. The well wagon was constructed in 1998 and is not a common visitor to the MER (20 Decmber 2018)

Left: the ballast hopper borrowed from the steam railway (see photograph on page 82), which arrived on the MER in the previous November, heads south past Dreemskerry in the charge of diesel-electric locomotive 34 (8 January 2015)

Below: also seen heading south past Dreemskerry is the yellow tippler wagon. The start of the operating season was in four days' time, on 28 March 2015. Over the winter of 2014-5, Ballure Viaduct was refurbished (see pages 20-1) and it is likely that engineering stock is being moved to clear the line before normal service resumes. Motor car 33 is hauling the wagon (24 March 2015)

A second flat wagon may usually be found parked in the siding at Dhoon Quarry and, at the time of writing, partners 45. This vehicle was constructed in 1926 and carried the number 21 in the MER freight series. Over the years the vehicle has appeared in a variety of configurations. Originally a stone wagon, it lost its sides in 1962-3. 1.6ton (1600kg) hydraulic cranes were installed at each end in the mid-1970s to facilitate the loading and unloading of rails. It was converted to a ballast hopper wagon in 2000, finally reverting to a flat wagon, but without cranes in 2008. Interestingly, the trucks of this are Brush D trucks, presumed to be rescued from one of the motor cars lost in the Laxey shed fire in 1930.

A relatively recent addition to the active MER engineering stock has been a green-painted railcar, manufactured by Wickham of Ware in Hertfordshire, and its associated trailer. The railcar was built in 1956 and spent time on the Lochaber Narrow Gauge Railway in Scotland, arriving on the island in May 1978 after the closure of the Scottish line. It saw occasional use on the MER in the 1980s, but spent many years out

Right: the siding at Dhoon Quarry is regularly used by the engineering department. The tippler wagon is stabled here on the first day of the 2015 operating season. Unusually the handbrake wheel is near the centre of the wagon: on most vehicles they are found at the ends (28 March 2015)

Above: for a time between the 1950s and the 1970s car 1 was often used on works duties. Fitted with a basic windscreen, which provided the motorman with rudimentary weather protection, it stands outside Derby Castle shed with a weedkiller tank mounted on a wagon underframe (Courtesy, Travel Lens Photographic 1970s)

Left: in the early years of the twenty-first century car 7 was dedicated to engineering use. It has arrived in Laxey station and, the trolley having been turned, it is about to shunt flat car 52 into the siding by the goods shed just beyond the Mines Tavern (now just 'The Mines'). Number 52 was later equipped as the wire car and tower wagon (Sara Goodwins 7 May 2003)

Above: car 25 has been out on works duties and is returning to Ramsey car shed (demolished in 2016; see page 13) at the end of the day for overnight stabling. The legend 'Isle of Man Railways' is carried on the nameboard located on the car bodyside. A number of sleepers and a pickaxe are carried on the wagon. The conductor guides the trolley-head through the overhead frog (8 May 1996)

Right: car 27 has probably attended a minor overhead defect, on the Ramsey side of Laxey, with the tower wagon early one morning. With the tower wagon being pushed, they are now returning to Laxey shed, before the first scheduled service. Note the basic weather protection added to the motorman's platform of number 27 (6 May 1996)

Left: unusually tunnel car 9, identifiable by the illuminations scheme it is carrying, is on works duties. Flat car 45 is being shunted at Dhoon Quarry sidings and the pair are seen from the rear of a passing service car. The next southbound car is due shortly, after which car 9 and 45 will probably emerge from the siding to their worksite (12 May 2007)

Left: freight wagon 21 seen with the ballast hoppers in place at Ballafayle (Corteen). Directly behind the pole a member of staff is controlling the discharge of new ballast with the handwheel. Having been loaded at Dhoon Quarry, the wagon has been brought here by car 7, which is almost obscured by the hoppers. The chalked 'mobile café' notice seems wishful thinking. This view is taken from the rear of a northbound service car (8 May 2001)

Below: during 2018, winter saloon 21 had reliability problems with recurring hot boxes. For the latter part of the season it was not used in passenger service. Car 21 is passing Dreemskerry with the wire car, 52, having been used by the engineers to make a minor overhead repair near Lewaigue prior to the day's scheduled passenger service. The use of a winter saloon on engineering duties is very unusual (24 July 2018)

of use in the Isle of Man Railway's goods shed at Castletown. Following a major overhaul it returned to the MER for engineering use in July 2014. This railcar and trailer, being powered by a diesel engine, can operate independently of the electrical power. A gang of staff may be carried on the railcar itself, with small loads on the trailer and this makes it useful for accessing work sites remote from road crossings.

Currently stored out of use in the loading dock at Dhoon Quarry are three side-tipping wagons of 2.5 ton capacity (see top photograph on page 90). These were constructed by W. G. Allen of Tipton in the early 1940s for the Lochaber Narrow Gauge Railway, the same line that the Wickham Railcar originally served. The Lochaber line closed in 1977 and the side-tipping wagons came to the MER in 1997 after a period of private ownership. Painted in black, these three wagons are believed to have last been used in 2009, since when they have languished in the sidings at Dhoon Quarry.

The MER has also used a yellow-painted four-wheel low-floor wagon. This was originally brought to the Isle of Man for use in connexion with the IRIS sewerage scheme at the beginning of the twenty-first century. The IRIS scheme involved laying a pipeline under much of the steam railway, and required the temporary closure of parts of the line. The wagon was transferred to the MER in 2012 for use in updating the small sewage works at The Garey (near Dhoon Church). After this the wagon was often used in conjunction with trackside clearance and maintenance duties when quantities of cut bushes and trees were moved from the lineside for disposal. Originally a drop side wagon it was converted to a tippler for permanent way use, and worked in this guise between 2014 and February 2016, when it was transferred to the steam railway.

In previous years the engineers have used members of the passenger fleet as their dedicated vehicles. Cars 1 and 2 spent many years used in this way, and in the 1990s so were open motor cars 25 and 27. In the early part of the twenty-first century car 7 spent several years on engineering duties. Sadly car 7 was not adequately maintained during this time, spending a lot of time stored overnight at either Dhoon Quarry or in the roofless shed at Laxey with no weather protection. Eventually a major reconstruction of the car body became necessary before it could be returned to passenger service, which took place in 2011. The use of other cars for occasional engineering duties is not unknown. During 2018 winter saloon 21, repainted in the historic nationalized green and white livery, had recurring problems with hot boxes which severely affected its reliability in public service. Unusually, this winter saloon was employed on wire-car duties during the latter part of the 2018 season. Meanwhile, car 33 proved very popular during the Manx drought of that year. (Yes, there was a drought with a hosepipe ban in the Isle of Man!)

MER road vehicles

The provision of road vehicles is straightforward; small vans and pick-up trucks are stock items from commercial vehicle suppliers. The Manx government can make economies of scale with bulk orders across other departments such as highways and utilities. Access to site is not generally a problem as, except for a few stretches of the line, there are parallel roads close to the MER, and materials and personnel can be despatched from Derby Castle or Laxey, and be on site in well under an hour. Typical tasks handled by the staff and the small fleet of road vehicles include 'gardening' tasks at the stops, attention to trackwork - lubricating points and switches, etc.; painting of shelters; posting timetables and attending to trams which have developed minor problems while in service. One of the more common requests for assistance is to replace a worn trolley wheel: parking a van alongside the affected tram provides a working platform from the van roof, and allows the rapid replacement of the defective brass item (see page 74).

Above: as an alternative to the wire car the overhead engineers have the use of a cherry picker, HMN-290-T, which is here seen in action near Dreemskerry Farm. Note the splice ear on the end of the wire on the left is alreqady in place to be connected to a new section of wire. The cherry picker can be manoeuvred out of the way of service cars when necessary. Single-line working is, of course, in operation (17 April 2016)

Slightly less prosaic is the cherry-picker, which can be driven along the line if needed, and allows the overhead maintenance team to access defective equipment. The cherry-picker can often be seen parked near the overhead engineers' base in the old electrical substation between the car shed and the station at Laxey. A relatively frequent defect in the overhead is the failure of the contact wire due to fatigue: each passage of a tram causes flexing of the contact wire at every line ear. Wear reduces the wire cross section, and eventually breakage occurs at the peak stress point where the wire is clamped by the line ear (see also pages 78-9). Generally, the fallen wire will be earthed through the rails and the circuit breaker will switch off the power, stranding the tram. At the very least the overhead wire crew will need to splice in an extra length of new wire.

Dewirements of moving trams can also cause problems. At higher speeds the dynamic forces increase, as does the probability of dewirement, something which all motormen are aware of. The first sign of dewirement is that the sprung trolley pole rises sharply: if the conductor is on the back platform then he should be able to retrieve the pole by hauling in the rope. The driver should bring the tram to an immediate halt. Otherwise there is a danger that the trolley head may catch on span wires or bracket arms causing impact damage to either the trolley and/or the overhead. It is not unknown for the trolley pole to be pulled from the tram after the trolley head has been ensnared in this way. Following

Left: the form of a splice ear used to connect two sections of round section wire. This example is near Dolland (16 September 2011)

Below: splices for the newer grooved wire are very different as they must transmit the higher axial tension forces present in this form of overhead. The top sections of the wires are clamped with a screw connector. On the right, the end of the existing wire is already clamped, while a ratchet device has been used to tension the new wire on the left. The overhead engineers are walking back along the line to check that the newly-unreeled wire is correctly aligned before they cut it to length and clamp it into place. (10 May 2018)

Below: the clamp in the previous photograph is now installed and carrying the required tension loads (10 May 2018)

a dewirement the crew walks back to carry out a visual check for damage and report any concerns for the attention of the overhead engineers. Until repairs are carried out there may be a temporary speed restriction at the affected pole(s), notification over the radio of extra care being needed at pole X being very quick and easy. For minor damage, which does not involve serious disruption to the service, the wire car and crew usually attend and carry our repairs next morning, before normal service starts.

Standard tractors are also in common use. Hedge- and verge-cutting equipment is fitted and used in a similar way as for highway maintenance, with the road wheels straddling the track. Such tasks can be carried out between service cars. The tractors are also fitted with towbar attachments and can be used to position the wire car, number 52, beneath bracket arms during installation of stretches of new overhead. Conductors are kept aware, by radio, of the location of the tractor, or other road vehicles, on the line and inform the motormen where they must proceed with due caution.

The Isle of Man Railways, i.e. the MER and the steam line, jointly operate a standard open tipper lorry. This is used for carrying bulk quantities of material, such as ballast and sleepers to site; removal of waste for disposal, etc.

When external contractors are employed to carry out track relay works, then provision of suitable vehicles including lorries, diggers, cranes and road rollers (used for trackbed consolidation) is part of the contract and they are brought to, and removed from, site as required by the contractors. Specialist equipment may be brought to the island, although the hire of plant from local specialists is also common. The use of road-railer vehicles has developed in recent years and these are particularly useful for accessing parts of the line remote from road access.

There has also been a move to using local storage sites for construction material in recent years. One example was the use of part of a field at Lewaigue in 2017 when track renewal between Lewaigue and Bellevue was under way. A storage site was also created on tramway property adjacent to the sharp curve between Ballig and Ballasholague during track relaying works during 2018. Site access was created by breaking through the wall on the main road.

Snaefell Mountain Railway

The logistics of access to the Snaefell Mountain Railway for maintenance purposes are less straightforward than those of the MER. There are no parallel roads, and access is only available at Laxey and the crossing of the A18 Mountain Road adjacent to The Bungalow Station. The majority of the line is laid at a gradient of 1 in 12 (8.33%), with the consequence that moving any equipment or material up or down the line requires extra care. The risk of any runaway is considerable. In order to minimise the likelihood of such accidents, any railed wagon is always propelled

Snaefell car 5 is in charge of the Hurst Nelson four-wheel wagon just below The Bungalow, showing the use of a passenger car on non-passenger duties. The wagon is uphill of the tram so cannot run away. It appears that there was no crossover here at that time. Car 5's body was destroyed by fire on 16 August 1970 and a replacement body now graces this vehicle (Courtesy, Travel Lens Photographic 1969)

There appears to be a special event taking place at the Snaefell depot. Car 3 and 4 stand outside the depot while the first Air Ministry Wickham railcar, painted in RAF blue, is displayed on the right (George Hearse, Courtesy Travel Lens Photographic, June 1956)

Snaefell freight tram 7, Maria, *is supported on barrels at the end of the siding by the depot. After the end of the winter season the trucks have been run out and returned to its donor passenger car. The tower wagon and the truck are available for use when required (Courtesy Travel Lens Photographic 20 June 1951)*

up the mountain with the power car on the downhill side of the vehicle (see top photograph opposite). The full braking capacity of the car is available to restrain the wagon and any load carried, and the tension capacity of any coupling is never relied on.

The Snaefell Mountain line sees far more non-passenger traffic than the MER, as the railway is the only practical means of reaching the summit of Snaefell. The National Air Traffic Services (NATS) radio station on Snaefell is a key component of British Air Traffic Control, and the transmitter equipment is housed in a large industrial building to the north east of the summit station. In addition, antennae serve the island's mobile telephone and radio networks. The

The Wickham railcars are visible, the larger 1957 vehicle is inside the shed, while the original stands outside. Both are wearing the black and yellow livery of the CAA. On the right is the 1895 Snaefell depot with its two roads. The overhead gantry carries an unusual twisted pair of wires, only practical with bow or pantograph collection. The siding beside the shed hosts the now grounded body of Maria, *the tower wagon and the open wagon (Courtesy Travel Lens Photographic, 14 August 1972)*

Summit Hotel, conveniently located by the summit station, provides refreshments when the tramway is operating, and evening dining during the operating season. All supplies for the NATS station, the hotel, the equipment for the telephone antennae and radio transmitters, and any staff and equipment have to be carried to and from the summit by the railway. The first tram up the mountain in the morning is not an advertised public service but brings staff and supplies for the Summit Hotel. This tram is also available for maintenance staff of the other facilities, and the transfer of equipment and people from van to tram takes place at The Bungalow Station, often taking several minutes. The final downhill tram in the evening returns the hotel staff, maintenance workers and equipment, as well as any rubbish for disposal.

Right: a beautiful spring day, but the Snaefell Mountain Railway has not yet opened for the tourist season. At the end of a day's work, the NATS Wickham railcar has descended from the summit and disgorged a team of workmen at The Bungalow to rejoin their road vehicles. The railcar driver has crossed the mountain road, closed the gates and heads downhill to Laxey (14 April 2010)

Snaefell car 6 has been transferred back to its own bogies in Laxey station and is being towed by back to the depot by car 5. Car 6's bow collectors and the sliding windows of the passenger saloon will need to be refitted before the car can be tested and returned to service. Car 5 had a new body constructed in 1971 to replace that destroyed by a fire in August 1970 (Courtesy Travel Lens Photographic May 1986)

In the siding by the Snaefell car shed (see photograph on page 99) the mountain line's four-wheel wagon, supplied by Hurst Nelson, is parked next to the tower wagon. Beyond is the now rather decrepit bodywork of the freight tram, car 7, Maria. The SMR tower wagon is mounted on a four-wheel underframe and comprises an elevated platform with a climbing frame for access.
(Courtesy Travel Lens Photographic 1960s)

The radio station on Snaefell was constructed by the Air Ministry in 1950. Control passed to the National Air Traffic Control Services (NATCS) when it was established in 1962. NATCS became part of the Civil Aviation Authority (CAA) when it assumed reponsibility from the Air Ministry in 1972, at which time the operator's name was shortened to NATS. As a Public-Private Partnership NATS separated from the CAA in 2001.

Although passenger traffic on the Snaefell line is seasonal, NATS provides continuous year-round air traffic control and it has alternative means of access to the radio station during the closed period, by arrangement with the railway. The first, petrol driven, railcar was acquired in 1951 and painted in RAF blue, carrying the Air Ministry insignia. This was joined by a second railcar in 1957, which was originally painted in a similar livery. After 1966 the livery was changed to black and yellow. Further railcars were acquired by NATS in 1977 and 1991, both of these remain operational, with the 1977 car acting as a back up to the newer one. The two older cars are no longer on the SMR. The railcars are stabled in their own brick-built shed adjacent to the Laxey car shed on the Snaefell line. The Wickhams each have a crew compartment and an equipment-carrying area with a crane. They are painted yellow and although not railway assets are essential pieces of equipment used by a third party on the mountain.

Prior to 1995 the Snaefell car bodies were overhauled at Derby Castle, with transfer to and from the MER taking place on the mixed gauge siding in Laxey. Upon return from overhaul the renovated trams were then towed uphill and shunted back into the depot where the electrical connexions were restored and testing took place before the car was released for further service.

Due to the broader gauge of the Snaefell line it requires its own dedicated engineering stock and does not share these with the MER, or indeed the steam railway. These vehicles are normally stabled at the Laxey depot and propelled by one of the passenger cars as required: unlike the MER there is no one car which is preferred by the engineers. In

At the end of the line at Snaefell summit an open wagon awaits its next call to duty. A close examination of the axle boxes (see inset) reveals their origin to be Milnes of Birkenhead. The wagon body is built on the underframe of one of the original car bogies, rendered spare after new bogies were fitted when the motor cars were re-equipped in the 1970s, This one continued in more humble use (6 May 2001)

Below: during the long dry summer of 2018 the Snaefell well ran low so water supplies were ferried up the mountain from Bungalow. Here a cubic metre tank is filled from a bowser ready to be propelled to the summit. The truck has no brakes but is held by passing a scaffold pole through the spokes. (10 August 2018)

During the 'Wartime on the Railways' event this 'crashed Spitfire' was set in a diorama at the summit of Snaefell. The wings have already been detached and the fuselage is in the process of being moved back to the tramway. The downhill journey will be on an SMR wagon with transfer to lorry at The Bungalow. Storage locations vary but it spent the previous winter in Ramsey bus garage (16 September 2016)

addition, the SMR has a simple open truck which appears to be based on the framework of one of the original 1895 bogies of the electric car fleet.

During the 'Wartime on the Railways' weekend, held annually on the Island's railways, a 'crashed Spitfire' is usually located somewhere near one of the lines to provide a diorama of World War II life. In 2016 this large, but less than full-size, model was located just below the summit station on the Snaefell line. Like everything else on the summit, it had been brought up by the tramway and, of course, had to be removed by the same means. A small tracked digger was used to move the model from the 'crash site' for loading onto a wagon, appropriately enough in pieces. The Spitfire is stored over the winter and has been seen in some unlikely places, including Ramsey bus garage.

Following the bad storms of December 2015, major work was needed on the Snaefell line and the contractor used a Thwaites road-railer vehicle to carry materials to and from The Bungalow. This vehicle has both flanged railway wheels and tyred road wheels which can be raised or lowered to change the modus operandi. The use of such engineering vehicles is common on UK main lines, but it was only in 2018 that one was recorded on the MER, operated by the contractor TXM on a track relay near Dhoon Quarry. The 3'-6" gauge road-railer accessed the line at The Bungalow, and was used to carry materials to the work site located about a mile downhill.

The maintenance of the MER and SMR continues to evolve. Modern working practices, with mechanized plant, have been introduced and have much in common with main line practice in the UK. This is not surprising, as much of the work is now carried out by UK-based contractors. The seasonal nature of the railway operations means that the engineers are not restricted by possession limitations for major work items, which can be carried out during normal working hours in the closed season. The Manx weather is rarely so extreme as to make winter working impossible.

A rather ungainly looking road-railer vehicle is in the siding at The Bungalow during winter engineering works. A Fell rail is about to be carried downhill for installation. A jacking mechanism can raise or lower the vehicle's road wheels for transition between modes. An articulation midway along the vehicle allows it to be steered on road, but this is locked in the straight position for use on track (16 February 2017)

ACKNOWLEDGEMENTS

The historic photographs have been mainly drawn from the collections held by Travel Lens Photographic. The assistance of Tony Wilson is gratefully acknowledged.

For her understanding during the collection and preparation of the material, editorial guidance, typesetting and bringing this book to its final printed form the assistance of my wife, Sara Goodwins, has been invaluable.

SELECTED BIBLIOGRAPHY

Basnett, Stan, *Mann Ablaze*, Leading Edge, 1991
Basnett, Stan, *Trams of The Isle of Man 1946-Present Day*, Lily Publications, undated c. 2008
Edwards, Barry, *The Manx Electric Railway*, B&C Publications, 1998
Edwards, Barry, *The Railways and Tramways of the Isle of Man*, Oxford Publishing Co., 1993
Edwards, Barry, *Trains and Trams of the Isle of Man*, Lily Publications, 2010
Goodwins, Sara, *Two Fish for the Summit*, Loaghtan Books, 2017
Goodwyn, Mike, *All about The Manx Electric Railway*, Manx Electric Railway Society, 1989
Goodwyn, Mike, *Douglas Head Marine Drive and Electric Tramway*, Manx Electric Railway Society, 1978
Goodwyn, Mike, *Manx Electric*, Platform 5 Publishing, 1993
Gray, Edward, *Manx Railways and Tramways*, Sutton Publishing, 1998
Heavyside, Tom, *Douglas – Laxey – Ramsey*, Middleton Press, 2010
Hendry, Robert P., *Manx Electric Railway Saga*, Adam Gordon, 2010
Hendry, R Preston and Hendry, R Powell, *Manx Electric Railway Album*, Hillside Publishing Co., 1978
Hobbs, George, *By Whing to Port Soderick*, Loaghtan Books, 2015
Hobbs, George, *Manx Electric Railway, Past & Present*, Loaghtan Books, 2014
Hobbs, George, *Stops Along the Manx Electric Railway*, Loaghtan Books, 2014
Hughes, Edward; Hiley, John; McKenzie-Smith, Ian, and Brown, Keith, *Hughes Electrical & Electronic Technology (twelfth edition)*, Pearson Education Limited, 2016
Iles, D.C., *Design Guide for Steel Railway Bridges*, The Steel Construction Institute, 2004
Jones, Norman, *Isle of Man Tramways*, Foxline Publishing c 1993
Pearson, F.K., *Isle of Man Tramways*, David and Charles, 1970
Pearson, Keith, *One Hundred Years of The Manx Electric Railway*, Leading Edge Press and Publishing, 1992
Terzaghi, Karl; Peck, Ralph B., and Mesri, Gholamreza, *Soil Mechanics in Engineering Practice (third edition)*, John Wiley & Sons Inc, 1996
Wilson, Ernest and Lydall, Francis, *Electrical Traction* (revised edition), Edward Arnold, 1907

Journals and periodicals

Manx Transport Review, Manx Electric Railway Society, various issues
Trams Magazine, Train Crazy Publication, various issues

Car 14 had been in long term storage in Ramsey shed until 2014 (see page 14), but a concerted effort by staff and volunteers saw her returned to service in September 2018. With three months to go before her unveiling, refurbishment is under way at Derby Castle (3 June 2018)